Becoming
Mama-San
80 Years of Wisdom

Mary Matsuda Gruenewald

NewSage Press
Troutdale, Oregon

BECOMING MAMA-SAN: 80 YEARS OF WISDOM
Copyright © 2013 Mary Matsuda Gruenewald
Paperback Original ISBN 978-0-939165-62-9

NEWSAGE PRESS
PO Box 607
Troutdale, OR 97060-0607
503-695-2211

www.newsagepress.com

Cover and interior design by Sherry Wachter.
www.sherrywachter.com

Printed in the United States.
This book is also available as an ebook.
Distributed to bookstores by Perseus Books
(Publishers Group West).

Library of Congress Cataloging-in-Publication Data
Gruenewald, Mary Matsuda, 1925-
Becoming mama-san : 80 years of wisdom / by Mary Matsuda
Gruenewald.
pages cm
Includes bibliographical references.
ISBN 978-0-939165-62-9 (alk. paper)
1. Gruenewald, Mary Matsuda, 1925- 2. Conduct of life. I. Title.
> BJ1547.5.G78A3 2013
> 170'.44--dc23
> 2013006038

1 2 3 4 5 6 7 8 9 10

For Mama-San

Acknowledgments

With new projects come new reasons for feeling grateful and expressing appreciation. I continue to feel supported and cared for by my writing teacher, Brenda Peterson, and my publisher, Maureen R. Michelson, as well as my classmates Meredith Bailey, Kathryn Barrett, Pamela Dodson, and Kimberly Richardson, among others.

My special thanks to Miyoko Matsuda, my sister-in-law, and Martha Matsuda, my daughter, for accompanying me to Japan in 2006 (among many other reasons). My hosts in Japan made extraordinary efforts on my behalf. Thanks to Donna Fujimoto in Osaka; Marie Tsuruda, Caroline Lloyd, and Naomi Fujishima in Hiroshima; and Samantha Lim at the Tokyo American Club. Masako Iino laid the foundation for my trip two years earlier, and visiting her at Tsuda College was one of many highlights of the trip. My friend Yoshiko Koga-san gave generously of her time, including guiding us on an amazing tour of Tokyo to visit important historical sites.

Meeting my relatives from Japan for the first time was a life-altering experience for me. The generosity of Muneaki Horie and his wife, Kayoko, was astounding. It was also a pleasure to meet their two sons, Munekazu and Toshihiro. We went with them as their guests to the famous Buddhist monastery at Koyasan for a vegetarian meal, a tradition Japanese public bath, and overnight accommodations on traditional Japanese futons. Most amazing of all was meeting Muneaki's mother, Shizuko Horie. Being received into her home was like meeting the sister I never had.

Hiroshi and Sadako Kashiwagi, and their son, Soji, came into my life at the perfect moment. We helped each other heal our final wounds from the internment experience, and we remain close friends.

I get much of my energy from my special friends, some of whom I have known for decades: Wendy Noritake, Glenda Pearson, Linda Ando, Jan Crosman, and especially John Runyan. I thank all of you for your kindness and support.

It has been a privilege watching my four nieces grow into fine role models: Marlene Fong, Kathryn Nagao, Marguerite Sandico, and Sheila Chan. You and your families are a delight and an ongoing source of joy for me.

As for my immediate family, I couldn't be more grateful. Martha, David, and Ray, I am incredibly proud of each of you as you continue on your life journeys, being true to yourselves. I have enjoyed watching you develop into wonderful human beings, from the time you were born until now, as I move into my elder years. My deepest thanks go to my brother Yoneichi, my father Papa-san, and of course, Mama-san. They are all long-since deceased, but they still live in my heart and continue to teach me life's most important lessons.

Contents

Becoming Mama-san

$\mathcal{I}$t was a perfect midsummer evening on Vashon Island, a short ferry ride from Seattle, and Mount Rainier was glowing a beautiful pink to the southeast of our farm. This was the very best time of the year for Mama-san and I to savor the beauty of the fields, when the harvest was complete and we had time to reflect. She liked to pass on her appreciation for life during our walks.

"I am so grateful that the harvest went well this year," she said, in her formal Japanese. "Do you remember how hard the four of us worked this spring?"

From where we were standing, we could look around and see all ten acres of our farm. Tidy rows of strawberry plants covered gently rolling hills. Our modest farmhouse stood in one corner of the property, with the barn nearby.

"I am very proud of how well you and Yoneichi-san worked together," Mama-san added. "Now, you can see that it all paid off."

She sighed with contentment as her eyes swept over the landscape. Her smile was all I ever needed to feel secure and seen.

As we turned to continue our walk, a flash of red in the next row over caught my attention. I bent down and parted the green leaves. "Look, there's one for each of us."

I handed her the larger of the two, last-of-the-season berries and we ate them, nodding at each other.

My mother, Mitsuno Horie Matsuda, was the kindest, wisest person I have ever met. I spent my childhood wanting to please her. As a young adult, I rebelled against her, and against her culturally-based expectations for me. More recently, and especially since her passing in 1965, I have tried to become as much like her as I possibly can.

Mama-san was born in 1892 in Japan, a proud and ancient culture. In 1922, she married my father and came to America, intending to live and die here. In *Looking Like the Enemy*, I wrote of how my mother's wisdom rescued me from the depths of despair during my most challenging times in the Japanese-American concentration camps. In the most difficult of circumstances, she remained amazingly resilient and optimistic, even while those around her felt hopeless. When my publisher asked me to write another book, I knew that my mother would be its focus.

Mama-san's wisdom developed and deepened while she raised a family, earned a living through hard physical labor, and faced severe discrimination in her adopted country. It was only as I pondered the materials for this book that I came to fully appreciate the elegance of her beliefs and how important a role model she could be—not just for me, but for others as well. As I observe the 21st century begin to unfold, the power of her message from the 19th century seems more applicable than ever.

—MARY MATSUDA GRUENEWALD
January 2013

Author's Note

*L*ike most of my peers, I have always used the phrase "intern-ment camps" as a polite way of describing the confinement of me, my family, and tens of thousands of other Japanese Americans during World War II. In July, 2012, I attended a meeting of the National Japanese American Citizens League in Bellevue, Washington. Professor Lane Hirabayashi and activist Martha Nakagawa gave convincing arguments for the use of the term "concentration camps" instead of "internment camps." I realized that I need to use accurate vocabulary to more honestly label the experience and not shy away from uncomfortable truths. I would like to thank the people who had the courage to press this issue, and I have incorporated the new terminology in this book.

Becoming
Mama-San

CHAPTER ONE

The Privilege of a Simple Life

My family lived the American dream in the early years of my life. Not the modern version of glittering excess that is often portrayed in the media, but the original dream that the founders of this country would have recognized. My family had a sense of considerable freedom living in a democratic society, with far more opportunity than we would have had anywhere else. We were grateful to work hard and better our lives. Ours is a story of an immigrant family that worked steadfastly, endured hardship, and made any sacrifice necessary to fully participate in everything this country has to offer. My parents felt fortunate to raise their children in the United States. Over the years, we would not be deterred, even when our country turned against us.

I was born in Seattle, Washington in 1925. Some people might think of my childhood as impoverished because by today's standards, I did not have a financially privileged life.

Instead, what I had was a rich environment full of natural beauty, the opportunity to explore and learn through direct experience, and a chance to develop self-reliance. My parents' gratitude for simple things was key to their worldview—one that eventually became my worldview. They passed on wisdom that, to this day, has given me the strength to transcend life's ordeals.

My father, Heisuke Matsuda, was born in 1877. Papa-san was fifteen years older than my mother, Mitsuno. In the Japanese-American community, they were known as *Isseis*, first generation immigrants, born in Japan. My brother, Yoneichi, was two years older than I, and we were called *Niseis*, born in the United States, and therefore, we were American citizens.

My earliest memories were of a modest life at our first home on Vashon Island, about a twenty-minute ferry ride from Seattle. My parents rented an old drafty house in the country where the curtains waved in the breeze even when the house was completely closed up. The house sat in a wooded area on a flat plateau. Below us was Puget Sound to the southeast, but all we could see were trees. Our two neighbors lived about a mile away, and I had no regular playmates other than Yoneichi.

We didn't have electricity, which for rural areas was still something of a luxury in the 1920s. We pumped cold water by hand from a well located outside the back door, and heated it over a wood stove, which also heated the house. We took baths in a primitive galvanized tub in the middle of the kitchen floor.

An outhouse situated fifty feet out the back door was our bathroom, no matter the season.

Our lives revolved around our immediate neighborhood, a much smaller area than most people operate in now. Our family farm and home were located on the same piece of land. We bought groceries from a store down the road, about one mile away. We raised chickens and had a goat that provided milk. We grew much of what we needed to eat. We walked everywhere since we had no car. Cars were not readily available in my childhood, but we didn't need them either. We had no radio, telephone, TV, or refrigerator, not even an icebox. Despite our lack of conveniences, we were content.

You could say we had a richness of place and family, but not things! Our only toys were a tricycle for Yoneichi and a kiddy car for me. Nature and miles of wide-open countryside surrounded our home. In those early years, nature was our main source of wealth, providing a means to grow our food and make a livelihood. It also fed our souls with its beauty, and provided me with many vivid life lessons.

One of my earliest memories was when I was about four years old. One hot, muggy afternoon, I was sleeping on my bed while my parents worked outside. Thunder woke me up and I rushed to the back door just in time to see lightning strike the top of a tall Douglas fir nearby. A raging ball of fire raced down the entire side of the tree, peeling off the bark before it plunged into the ground with a deafening BOOM that shook the house. Rain followed in torrents, soaking my parents as they scurried from the fields back to the house. Trembling, I stood frozen on the back step.

"Mary-san!" my mother shouted, breathless, as she swooped me up in her arms and rushed inside. We were both shaking.

What I remember some 80 years later is that in my moment of sheer terror, my mother and father were there to comfort and protect me. A feeling of safety imprinted on every cell in my body. This would be the first of many times I remember my parents being there for me —a knowing I would hold onto for a lifetime.

Nature's power, whether it was giving or taking, influenced me profoundly in my early years. One time, my parents were taking the long loganberry canes and winding them between two rows of wire that had been strung for this purpose. They were worried because a wildfire was burning on the island. While they worked, I swung on the wire and prayed out loud to God: "*Kami sama, ame oh fu'te kudasai. Faya oh keyasa nai kara.*" "God, please make it rain because we have to put out the fire!"

To my surprise and delight, it rained that night. Years later, Mama-san talked about this incident, reminding me, "It rained hard enough that by morning the fire was out! Amazing what the earnest prayers of a little child can do!"

On warm summer days, we walked about a mile down the hill to the shores of Puget Sound. The beach was covered with a variety of shells, colored rocks, and driftwood, which

I collected and arranged in designs on the beach, only to have the high tide wash them all away. I liked playing with different kinds of crabs and watching them run sideways away from me. Sometimes, we would bring a bucket and dig for butter clams that Mama-san would later cook for dinner.

Once, I saw my parents walk down to the beach in their bathing suits and go for a swim. I could hardly believe my eyes. I didn't know they knew how to swim or even that they had swimsuits. Mama-san had tucked her black hair into a swimming cap and she looked trim and tanned. Papa-san had a farmer's tan with his face and neck much darker than the rest of his body. He was a small man, but solid and muscular from years of hard work. Laughing and calling to each other, they took big strokes away from me and lazily swam in the calm waters. It tickled me to see my parents playful and relaxed. Usually, they were too busy working in the berry fields, planning for the day they would own their own farm. This would be my only memory of seeing my parents swim.

My first home near the shores of Puget Sound was a Garden of Eden. Towering, thick, old growth trees bordered two sides of our home, creating a cathedral that opened to the sky. There were all kinds of places to explore at the beach and in the woods, ever-changing with the seasons. The world was my playground, and the birds, fish, snakes, and even angleworms were my playmates. In summer, I'd eat fresh fruit right off of the vine or low hanging branches—wild salmonberries, Italian plums, and crisp apples.

Despite the usual bumps and bruises of childhood, I felt completely safe in nature, and comforted. Nature would later become my refuge during those times when the world was harsh and unjust.

In early 1929, my father fulfilled a lifelong ambition by cashing in his life savings and buying ten acres of farmland near the center of Vashon Island. To this day, I am amazed by the wise and fortuitous timing of his decision, coming as it did shortly before the stock market crash of October 1929. He planned, worked, and saved for twenty-seven years before deciding the time was right.

Papa-san hired someone to build a four-bedroom house, and for two years during the start of the Great Depression he provided work and income for the island's hardware store, lumberyard, and tradesmen. In 1931, we moved into our new house, which had all of the modern conveniences of the time, including electricity, hot and cold running water, an indoor toilet that flushed, and a utility room. All of our friends and neighbors came to our first open house. Mama-san prepared sushi, teriyaki chicken, and teriyaki salmon. The new, extra long kitchen counter, built unusually low to accommodate Mama-san's five-foot stature, was brimming with even more food brought by our guests. It was an all-American potluck dinner with a Japanese twist!

Our new home wasn't extravagant, but compared to the one we had lived in, it was the height of luxury. Yoneichi and I even had our own separate bedrooms. The new house was much warmer in winter and cooler in summer. Our house was among the nicest of those owned by the Japanese families on the island. I was proud of this fact, but Mama-san had to remind me repeatedly not to brag about it.

The oil stove in the living room provided heat for the upstairs bedrooms through a vent in the ceiling. Mama-san cooked in the kitchen with a wood-burning stove. When it was time for chopping wood, all four of us pitched in. Papa-san split the huge chunks of wood in half or quarters. Yoneichi and Mama-san cut those pieces and split them to fit the kitchen stove. I had a small hatchet for making kindling from the larger pieces of wood. We all worked together and even as a small child I felt as though I was an important part of the effort.

The four of us, along with our horse Dolly, labored year-round, farming a variety of berries in those early years. Later, we specialized in strawberries, as my father found them to be the best crop. Every summer, he recruited workers of all ages from Seattle and Vashon to harvest the fruit, which was taken by truck to be processed into jam and jelly. As one of the island's chief employers of school-age children, he influenced many families in positive ways. Child labor was common back in the Depression era, and some of the families needed the income from their children's labor to buy essentials.

There was a pond in the next field over where Yoneichi and I played after the day's work was done. When we first moved into our new house, we didn't know the pond was there because it was hidden by tall grass and brush. It was a thrill when we first discovered it. Nearby, we found a crude raft and a long pole, so naturally we explored the pond's environs. I was always a little afraid of the unknown dangers I conjured up in my mind, lurking just below the pond's surface, but Yoneichi would often float about the pond by himself.

The pond was full of pollywogs in the spring, and later in the year we could hear the chorus of croaking frogs every evening. We would find clumps of eggs and bring them home in a jar and wait for the pollywogs to hatch. It was fascinating to watch them develop their legs and eventually turn into frogs. We never kept them until they matured, but instead returned them to the pond and let them go free. The pond was a treasure, a hidden preserve full of mystery and adventure, just for Yoneichi and me.

Spirituality was important to my parents, so Yoneichi and I joined the Vashon Methodist Church, which happened to be the first church we encountered on our walk into town. Papa-san and Mama-san didn't attend because their English wasn't good enough to follow the services, but Yoneichi and I quickly became comfortable there. When Mama-san first came to America, she moved on from the Shintoism of her youth and embraced Catholicism in her adopted country. But when Yoneichi and I began telling our parents about what we were learning at the Methodist church, Mama-san got curious, and soon, she and Papa-san joined the Japanese Methodist church in Seattle.

Occasionally, when the minister was available, my parents hosted services in our home for Japanese-speaking *Isseis* on the island. The services were Methodist, but the people who attended were of a variety of faiths, including Shinto and Buddhist. Another family on the island held occasional Buddhist services in their home, and we also attended those whenever we were invited. At the Methodist services, we sang hymns that I had learned in church. The *Isseis* sang in Japanese while I sang the same hymn in English. At the Buddhist services, I listened and had prayerful thoughts in English while the priest chanted, rang a gong, and lit incense in front of the altar. I couldn't understand what he was saying, but the atmosphere made it easy to pray to God.

I was comfortable in all of these situations. It felt perfectly natural for me to grow up in this mixed spiritual environment. I knew only that God is God of all of us, and the language, rituals, and even teachings didn't change that.

Cultural education was also important to my parents because they wanted us to retain a sense of our Japanese heritage. When I was in the eighth grade, they sent Yoneichi and me to kendo classes, where I was the only girl. Kendo is a martial art that requires full body armor and a padded helmet, and teaches discipline of mind, body, and spirit. My parents registered me for the class not only for the exercise and discipline but also for my posture. Whenever I walked, my head leaned out in front of the rest of my body. Kendo required me to stretch my arms back behind my head, forcing my posture to be more upright.

When we had learned enough of the basic strokes, we were told to put on all the armor for our first taste of combat. My heart was already beating briskly from the warm-up, but my whole body broke out in a sweat as my muscles tensed in preparation to fight. I was paired up with a boy a year older than me. At the word to begin, "*Hajime!*" he took a swift swing at the left side of my head. Stars flew, I heard ringing in my left ear, and I staggered to maintain my balance. I was stunned, not expecting him to act so quickly.

The teacher standing beside us shouted, "Raise your *shinai!* Defend yourself!" The boy hesitated. In that moment, I angrily and swiftly swung my *shinai* and hit him on the padding on the left side of his neck. I said to myself, *There, how do you like that?*

I felt satisfied that I had evened the match. That was the end of our encounter. After that, the teacher paired up other students to give each one a chance to engage in combat. Kendo gave me many things in life, including a sense of comfort and confidence during times of conflict. Thanks to kendo, I have had good posture ever since. And in the years and decades that followed, it allowed me to negotiate many battles with deftness and integrity.

Because we lived in such a small community, my grade school went from first through the eighth grade. I looked forward to the big step to high school, and though I was anxious, it was easier knowing that Yoneichi was already there.

About thirty-five of us attended the orientation for the incoming freshman class, where each girl was assigned a "big sister." Mine was a popular white girl named Bobbie, who was a senior. She put me at ease immediately, and introduced me to a number of girls and female teachers. I felt special having such an outstanding student as my "big sister." Later, I realized this honor may have been influenced partly by Yoneichi's high standing in the school. Maybe they expected me to follow in his footsteps.

In those days, I did not detect any racism on our island. Vashon High School was a melting pot in which Japanese-American students held leadership roles. We were well represented in the student government, the Honor Society, and sports. Yoneichi participated in all of these activities as the secretary of the student body, and as a short but fast player on the varsity football team.

High school presented the usual challenges for me, along with some that most of my Caucasian peers wouldn't expect. For the first time, students my age gradually started pairing off, but none of us Japanese-American students would dream of doing so. It just wasn't culturally acceptable to date, certainly at that age. It was an unspoken assumption in the Japanese culture that we would have arranged marriages, which made dating unthinkable. But for me and my Japanese peers, watching our classmates date opened us up to a whole new set of ideas. I began to wonder if an arranged marriage was best for me, and whether I could be happy in such a relationship.

At school, I found myself interested in a handsome, athletic white boy, and we enjoyed chitchatting with each other. I knew my parents would not approve, so mentally I kept him at arm's length. Still, I couldn't help but think about him, and I wondered what he thought about me.

One day, while we were preparing dinner together, I asked Mama-san, "Am I beautiful?"

She looked up at me briefly, surprised, and then turned back to the carrots she was chopping. "No, you're not," she replied, matter-of-factly. "But be grateful for the face you have. If you were too pretty, boys might pursue you for your looks alone. On the other hand, if you were ugly, they might avoid you because of that." Mama-san smiled at me and continued, "Be grateful for the face God gave you." Then she swept the carrots off the cutting board into a saucepan.

I looked down at the floor to keep from showing Mama-san that I was very disappointed, but deep down I knew she was right. If she had said that I was beautiful, I might have thought she was saying that to keep from hurting my feelings. I thought about what it would be like to be beautiful and glamorous, like Greta Garbo, Carole Lombard, or some of my other favorite movie stars. Wistfully, I imagined crowds cheering for me and asking for my autograph, knowing that it would never happen. As it was, I decided I had an ordinary looking face and a healthy, maturing body. I knew Mama-san loved me just the way I was, and that was enough. I could always count on her to be completely truthful with me.

My mother's blunt honesty was just one of many ways in which my parents demonstrated an unusually deep level of respect for me. Looking back, I think they were both quite extraordinary. While my mother and father were clearly products of their culture, they were also quite different from most of their peers in important ways.

My father treated his wife as an equal at a time when the Japanese tradition was that the husband made all of the decisions. His charm extended to the way he was quietly considerate of others. One of my adult friends recalled that Papa-san was the only one at community gatherings who brought special treats for all of the children, such as soda pop or candy. As a boss, when dozens of workers came to our farm to help with our harvest, he would give each of them candy at nine o'clock every morning. And to celebrate the end of the harvest, he bought ice cream for all of the workers and any of their family members who showed up—even during the height of the Depression.

Many Japanese fathers gave special attention to their oldest sons, and Papa-san clearly had expectations for Yoneichi that he didn't have for me. But Papa-san made me feel special, as well. When he and I ran errands together in Seattle or Tacoma, he always made it fun. When we went to Seattle to see the optometrist, we always went to Maneki's restaurant and had the same thing for lunch every time: miso soup, rice, and *buta dofu* (pork with tofu). After lunch, we would tour different stores, or visit a family friend, or have an ice cream soda.

My mother was the youngest of ten children. Her father died when she was only two, and her mother died when she was six. She ended up being raised by her adoring older siblings, who nurtured her and provided her with an education far beyond what most Japanese girls in that era received. Her outlook on life was always upbeat and positive, even in the most difficult of times.

As a family, we talked with one another more than most, and in a different manner. My parents were genuinely interested in my brother's and my daily lives, but I never felt like they were prying. I felt comfortable talking about school, my friends, or whatever else was on my mind. Sometimes, Mama-san or Papa-san told us of their early lives, including Papa-san's harrowing experiences, as a young man, of extreme prejudice. No topic was off limits.

Both of my parents had a sense of adventure and a relative lack of need for control. From a young age, I felt respected and loved by my parents. It did not matter that my wants and desires might change from one moment to the next, or that they might seem unimportant to an adult; my thoughts and opinions were still honored by them. Their guidance was gentle, and mostly by example, rarely verbal. Arguments were almost unheard of in my family. Punishments were meted out with care, but hardly seemed necessary except on the rarest of occasions.

Later, it was this degree of respect from my parents that ironically would allow me to deviate from the path that a Japanese daughter was expected to follow. My decision to marry a *hakujin* (white man) in 1951 created the only serious conflict between my parents and me. At that time, interracial marriages were rare in the United States. A strong but unspoken sense of cultural pride within the Japanese-American community implied that marrying outside of our community was "beneath" us.

As open and as generally accepting as my parents were, nothing prepared them for the shock that I delivered on the day I announced my engagement. It was a scandal that brought shame on my family. And yet, once their dismay wore off, my parents' values and respect for me would win out, overcoming their initial expectations that came from culture and precedent.

In accepting my husband into the family, my parents came to a new appreciation of the fundamental truth that all people are created equal, an ideal central to Americans. It is a simple concept, but one that is difficult to live up to in practice, especially during times of conflict, or when social norms interfere with our ability to understand and accept other people.

During World War II, my family suffered greatly at the hands of Americans who did not understand this fundamental truth. And because of the trauma I endured then, it would take a lifetime of affirming events for me to fully return to a belief in my own worthiness. I could not have made this journey, from the depths of depression back to acceptance, without the privileges I was afforded as a child—a simple life, close to nature; an emphasis on hard work and self-reliance; and the unconditional love and respect of my parents.

CHAPTER TWO

How Much Is Enough?

My father was one of many Japanese men who immigrated to the United States at the turn of the 20th century. He started with nothing, or even less than nothing, since he had to borrow money in order to pay for his passage from his native Japan to Hawaii. He was the fourth of five sons, and since Japanese tradition dictated that the oldest son inherited the family home and took care of the parents, Papa-san was free to seek his own way.

Papa-san was 18 years old when he left home, and in those days the only way to cross the Pacific Ocean was by ship—a long, expensive, and potentially hazardous journey. To pay for his passage to the United States, he initially worked in the sugarcane fields in Hawaii and in the coalmines in Alaska. Like most foreigners who didn't speak English well, Papa-san's opportunities were limited to minimum wage jobs with long hours and hard labor. And yet he seemed to thrive on this. When I was growing up, not once did I hear him complain about what must have been difficult years.

Part of the secret of Papa-san's success was that he actually enjoyed work. He took pride in doing even simple, repetitive jobs well, so he had little need to distract himself during his leisure time. His work ethic was not forced; it was part of who he was.

For several decades, Papa-san labored, first, to get out of debt, and second, to accumulate savings. Unlike many people at the time, he did not invest in the stock market; instead, he put his money into an account at a savings and loan. He also followed the advice of a friend and invested in a $1,000 New York Life Insurance policy as a way to earn additional funds over time. I often marveled at how he could be so focused on future gains, denying himself the pleasures that other single Japanese men engaged in. Many of them gambled, or drank to excess, or just daydreamed about future possibilities, but not Papa-san.

He had a goal: To find himself a Japanese bride who shared his vision of raising a family in America. He was not content to take his chances with a picture bride. Most of his peers selected their brides from a book of photographs, sparing themselves the huge expense of a round-trip voyage to Japan. Papa-san was patient, willing to wait, and work, for the most important decision of his life.

When Papa-san returned to Japan to select his bride, he employed the help of a *baishakunin* (go-between). Traditionally, a third party chose potential couples. This was to eliminate the possibility of diseases, insanity, or alcoholism in the marriage, to ensure matches were made with members of the appropriate class, and to keep both families happy with the outcome.

Even though my parents initially met with the assistance of a *baishakunin*, the two of them had an unusually long and honest first meeting. They discussed Papa-san's life in the United States and what each one might want from a life spent together in a new country. Traditionally, the man would have simply stated the terms of the relationship and expected his prospective bride to accept. It was unusual for Papa-san to consider his potential bride's opinion, much less for him to ask about her hopes and concerns as a peer.

As it turned out, my mother was adventurous and a good match for my father. She appreciated being treated as an equal partner and eagerly embraced my father's dreams. She really wanted to come to the United States, and was very happy with Papa-san's proposal to make America their permanent home. My parents were married in Japan in 1922, and came to the United States where they lived for the rest of their lives.

Mama-san was different from many other Japanese brides, some of whom arrived in the United States and were disappointed to discover that their new mates were lowly farmers or laborers. Few of the picture brides even knew what their husbands looked like before arriving here. Still, many young Japanese women preferred the risk of an anonymous marriage in a far-off country to the fate that could have awaited them back home. In the Japanese culture of the early 20th century, marrying a man usually meant living with him in his parents' home—and possibly enduring a life of servitude under both her husband and her in-laws. Traditionally, the bride was the lowest ranking member of the Japanese household with many responsibilities and few privileges.

The United States was attractive because of the promise of opportunity. Land was plentiful, and the news reaching Japan was that there were many prospects for making money in this young, rapidly growing country. However, Japanese immigrants could not know the difficulties that awaited them. For those brides brave enough to accept the proposals, their passage to this country, paid for by their husbands, was irreversible. Once here, some of the women felt stuck in unhappy situations with no reasonable alternatives. Out of necessity, they adopted an attitude of "*shikata ga nai*" (it cannot be helped) and "*gaman suru*" (persevere). This stoic acceptance of their situation would later prove critical during the hardships Japanese Americans would face during World War II.

In a sense, Mama-san was just as "stuck" as the other picture brides, except for her frame of mind: She understood and accepted the hardships of starting a new life, and chose to be happy with her decision. Together, they would handle any difficulties that might come their way.

In their early years together, they lived with other Japanese families in the Seattle area for social and financial support. This allowed them to continue to save for a few more years, and gave Mama-san a chance to adapt to her new environment and learn the farming profession. Living with others also provided a few more helping hands for raising my brother and me when we were infants. In time, they moved to a rented house on Vashon Island, and for the first time the two of them farmed the land by themselves.

By early 1929, Papa-san's savings had increased considerably and he could have kept his money invested, but he knew when he had enough. Papa-san cashed in his savings account and life insurance policy, bought our 10-acre farm, and built our house. He paid cash, which was more common in those days, prior to the development of the modern mortgage market.

My parents established a simple way of life when I was young, and we were mostly isolated from outside influences. As a child, I had no reason to want anything more than what I already had. Working every day, especially in spring, was a part of my childhood, but I didn't necessarily consider it work. It was just a part of being in my family. I didn't earn money for my efforts. As a child, money wasn't necessary or expected, and I'm not even sure it occurred to my parents to give me any. They already provided everything I needed. As a result, I never got into the habit of spending money in order to feel satisfied. And because I didn't have money, it was never a solution to any problem I may have had as a young person.

But as I grew up and went to school, I began to compare myself with other children. Gradually, I realized that some of them had things that I didn't. For the first time, I started developing yearnings beyond my basic needs.

Every fall, before the school year began, our family took the twenty-minute ferryboat ride to the mainland to buy school clothes for the year. This was a big adventure, and I really looked forward to shopping at Rhodes Brothers, a department store in Seattle. Sometimes, we'd shop at JC Penney. One year, when I was in the eighth grade, I found myself looking forward to clothes shopping more than the family outing. When we got to Rhodes, I immediately found an outfit that I just loved. It was a turquoise and magenta plaid jacket, a pleated magenta skirt, and a white blouse.

While Yoneichi and Papa-san went off to another part of the store, I continued to look at all of the other possibilities. Over and over again, I brought various combinations to show Mama-san. "Don't these look beautiful together?" I asked.

"Ah, very nice," she replied. "That would look very good on you."

Soon, I had quite a pile of outfits to consider. Eventually, I decided on three outfits and arranged them side-by-side. I was imagining the compliments my school friends would pay me if I were to wear each of them. Caught up in my thoughts, Mama-san finally called out to me in a quiet, questioning tone. "Mary-san?"

I looked over at her. She raised an eyebrow, and with a gentle, almost amused expression, asked, "How much is enough, Mary-san?"

The question caught me completely off guard. I stared at her, open-mouthed, for a long time. "I—I—I don't know," I said.

My cheeks flushed, and I looked away, embarrassed. When I glanced back at Mama-san, she gave me a reassuring smile and nod, and I felt better. She was still proud of me.

I turned back to the three outfits. Then I scanned the dozens of racks of clothes in the store, with hundreds of clothing choices. *How much,* I asked myself.

Mama-san could have just *told* me how much was enough, but then I wouldn't have had to think about it for myself.

Mama-san and Papa-san wore simple, serviceable work clothes day after day as they worked in the fields. They wore khaki work pants, long sleeve shirts, sturdy shoes, and a hat; that was all they needed. They each had a nice outfit for special occasions, but nothing more.

Did I really want a lot of nice clothes, which would only make my friends envious? I wondered.

I had always been taught not to show off, and I had certainly been tempted to do so, even right there in the department store. I decided I only needed two sets of new clothes. I still had nice clothes from previous years that were in good shape and still fit me. I kept my original choices, including the turquoise and magenta plaid jacket! On that day, I also learned to ask myself, *How much is enough?* A simple self-examination that has stayed with me a lifetime.

∞

My parents never bought more than they were able to afford and use. Even when our finances improved and we were fairly comfortable, they never wasted anything. Mama-san continued to save pieces of string to tie up sweet pea vines by the house or climbing pea plants in the vegetable garden. She saved paper bags that could be used again for another purpose. Coffee grounds and peelings from fruits and vegetables were buried in the garden. My parents didn't think of themselves as frugal. They just naturally recycled useful things. Back then, we didn't have a garbage service to take away our trash every week, so we found that reusing and recycling was easier than throwing things out.

My mother and father bought everything we needed with cash. Credit cards didn't exist in those days, but it wouldn't have made any difference. If my parents didn't have the money, they wouldn't buy at that time, and so they always stayed within their means. Their frugality was not forced, and neither did they ever express any sense of feeling deprived of any luxury.

In the course of their lifetimes, my parents accumulated few material possessions. Instead, they found something wonderful about the quiet pleasure of saving and living well within their means. Perhaps some of this came from their lives as farmers. Even today, professional farmers know that each year's crop is at the mercy of the weather and other forces beyond their control. Such uncertainty naturally tends to create a sense of restraint when it comes to money. They never know whether next year's crop will be a success or failure.

Of course, life today is much different than the life I led while growing up on Vashon. Yet, today, there is movement toward voluntary simplicity and rediscovering ways to live with fewer things and find greater happiness. Along the way, there are many unexpected benefits to reap: the pleasure of sharing our abundance with those in need, rediscovering the benefits of physical fitness, and enjoying "doing" rather than "having." This approach may seem new in modern times, but it isn't. What is old is now new again.

My parents instinctively understood this concept of voluntary simplicity. They would have been surprised to discover that people were writing books about a lifestyle they took for granted. They recognized what was needed in order to live a modest yet elegant life, close to the land, and they knew how much was enough.

CHAPTER THREE

The Doorway of Boredom

The sun had not yet come up. An early morning chill numbed our hands as we checked strawberry plants, looking for bright red berries hidden under the dark green leaves. The soft swishing of our hands parting the leaves was punctuated by the periodic plunk of berries as we tossed them into wooden carriers.

After a hearty, pre-dawn breakfast, my three young children and I had begun picking in the field just behind my parents' farmhouse. We had moved to Vashon Island for the summer to help Yoneichi with the harvest.

For a while, it was just Martha, David, Ray, and I. As the sun rose, other people started arriving, most of them workers from previous years, including entire sets of siblings. As we picked, we shared updates on our lives, bursts of laughter punctuating the buzz of our conversation. Many of the pickers had become our friends over the years, working together to harvest the bounty every summer.

Yoneichi pulled up in his green, 1957 Chevy flatbed truck, carrying a group of teenagers from Vashon who had come to help and make some money. Yoneichi jumped out of the cab and quickly took charge. It was the mid-1960s, and Yoneichi had long since replaced Papa-san as the boss of the farm, even though Papa-san continued to work.

The first day of the berry harvest was in full swing, with more than one hundred workers of all ages. We were a mix of humanity from a variety of socio-economic backgrounds—from older migrant workers to sons and daughters of middle-class families in Seattle and Vashon. For migrant workers, this was a way to support their families. For many of the kids, picking berries was the only practical way they could earn money over the summer. I was one of several "straw bosses" who roamed the fields, supervised the workers, and helped everyone stay focused on the harvest.

Most of the pickers were regulars who showed up nearly every day during the harvest, along with a steady stream of newcomers. There were four berry farmers on the island, and some workers would roam among the different farms. Workers collected the berries in carriers, and each carrier contained six boxes that were about six inches on a side and three inches deep. The carriers had handles to make them easier to lug around. When pickers brought the full carriers to the transfer station, Papa-san would transfer the berries to a stackable "flat," which held twelve boxes.

In exchange for their hard work, pickers got one ticket for each full carrier. The tickets could be exchanged for cash at the end of the day or at any time during the season. Over the course of the day, the stacks of strawberry flats grew impressively, a tribute to the land's bounty and the pickers' hard work. The sweet smell of strawberries was everywhere, but it was the strongest and most mouth-watering at the transfer station. No matter how many strawberries I ate, I never grew tired of that wonderful aroma.

Most days by mid-afternoon, it got pleasantly warm, but it rained on us at least a few times every summer. When it did, we kept right on picking. Sometimes, it got hot, sapping everyone's energy, so we cooled off by taking breaks at a large wooden water barrel that was towed to the field every day.

My children always admired the fastest pickers. One of the best was a gregarious young man named Duane, who one day nearly broke the record of forty-three carriers, falling just one carrier short. Records like this were always set early in the season because the first picking of the fields yielded the largest berries. By the third or fourth picking, it took everyone a lot longer to fill their carriers. To compensate, Papa-san gave out different colored tickets in exchange for full carriers of berries. Each was worth a different amount depending on the color, and the value rose over the course of the season, as the berries got smaller. We started with red tickets, worth 25 cents each. Yellow tickets were valued at 35 cents, and blue ones were worth 50 cents apiece.

While all of the pickers were motivated by money, a few also had an aesthetic sense for their work. Each time, they brought perfectly mounded carriers brimming with ripe, unbruised berries to the transfer station. Somehow, they transformed the simple, repetitive task of picking berries into a craft they took pride in.

Workers were required to pick the rows "clean"—that is, they were expected to pick all of the berries that were ripe, not just the largest ones. Adults got a whole row to themselves, but the children got one side of a row or the other. With the deep furrows plowed between the rows, my youngest, five-year-old Ray, could completely disappear behind the lush growth of the strawberry leaves.

Work always ended around three o'clock, when a large delivery truck arrived to pick up that day's harvest. Strong young men loaded the berry flats onto the truck, which then went to a nearby barreling plant. There, the fruit was processed, frozen, and later shipped back East, eventually being made into jam or topping.

The harvest lasted about six weeks, depending upon the weather. It was dirty, backbreaking work, even for young bodies.

My kids worked hard every day, up to ten hours a day, six days a week. Sometimes, they would complain. "Mom, I'm tired," Dave said. "I don't feel like doing this any more." His hands were stained red from the berries, his clothes covered in juice and dirt.

"Here, let me help you awhile," I said. I'd squat down with him at his row and help him fill his carrier much faster. As a straw boss, I did this with all of the workers over the course of the day. Picking with them for even a few minutes helped to sustain their efforts and renew their dedication.

I had my children save all of their tickets for the whole season in separate jars. They counted their tickets almost every night, and kept track of how many they earned from day to day. At the end of every summer, they each received a big payout in cash. This was their spending money for the entire year. After their first year of picking, in 1965, their father took them to the neighborhood bank where they opened up savings accounts and learned to keep track of their money. Martha was eleven years old and David was nine. We decided it was not too soon for them to learn—even for little Ray—how precious money can be.

After the initial excitement of the new season wore off, berry picking was a tedious, hard job, with low pay. To relieve the monotony, some of the young people brought portable AM radios. The fields echoed with the top hits of the day— "Yesterday" from the Beatles, "Satisfaction" by the Rolling Stones, and the Monkees' "I'm a Believer." The music lifted people's spirits, even though it got boring when the same songs played over and over again.

Not everyone coped well with the boredom. Some gave up, often on their first day. Others tried to scam the system in various ways, eventually getting caught and kicked out. Those who stuck with it developed different strategies for staying motivated, such as getting competitive, feeling the responsibility to earn a living, enjoying watching their earnings grow, or simply taking pride in doing a good job. Each of them had to come up with his or her strategy for coping with the inevitable boredom that came with the job.

As adults, my children have told me that the summers they spent picking berries were crucial to their success as adults. It taught them to persevere, which is a useful trait in virtually any career. They also learned the value of money and the satisfaction of knowing they *really* earned it.

Every job has its boring parts, and almost any job can get boring after awhile. However, I have come to appreciate that boredom is a crucial part of our personal growth. I am glad my children learned to grapple with boredom at such a young age.

Over the years, I have heard from a number of people who grew up working for my brother. All of them have said the same thing: picking berries taught them many important life lessons. Later on, they found that they were stronger and more resilient because they experienced and worked through the inevitable boredom that comes from repetitive hard work.

Extreme boredom was something I had to learn to deal with when I was a teenager, but my circumstances were due to extreme events of a world in crisis. Yet, like my children, my boredom ultimately shaped my life in positive ways.

On December 7, 1941, Japan bombed the U.S. Naval forces stationed at Pearl Harbor, Hawaii. The following day, the United States declared war on Japan and entered World War

II. It was a huge shock to the American people as a whole, but people of Japanese descent felt an even deeper fear.

In the weeks and months that followed, false rumors and panic spread about possible sabotage by Japanese people living in Hawaii and along the West Coast of the United States. Politicians, journalists, and others created a frenzy of anti-Japanese sentiment. The U.S. government enacted rules for Japanese living on the coast. The government limited our right to travel, and denied or limited our access to our bank accounts.

Based on these fears, President Franklin Delano Roosevelt signed Executive Order 9066 on February 19, 1942. All people of Japanese descent on the West Coast were to be evacuated from their homes and placed in what the government called "internment camps." We would soon learn that these were actually concentration camps where we were held against our will. Today, Japanese Americans consider these concentration camps, asserting that the word "internment" did not accurately describe the forced imprisonment.

This government order included my brother and me, even though we were U.S. citizens. Ultimately, around 120,000 people living in Washington, Oregon, California, and Arizona were sent to Japanese-American concentration camps, stripped of their rights as U.S. citizens and legal immigrants.

Those of us from Vashon were forced to leave our homes on May 16, 1942. My parents, Yoneichi and I joined other Japanese Americans for a three-day journey on a rickety old train, having no idea where we were going. When we arrived at our destination, I was shocked at the harsh scene before me. Three rows of barbed wire topped high fences that surrounded acres of plain, tar-papered barracks. Guards with machine guns became our jailers, constantly watching our every move from guard towers, even through the night with the help of rotating searchlights. I was 17 years old. Instead of finishing my junior year of high school, I was suddenly forced into an unimaginable nightmare.

The four of us slept on taut, canvas army cots in a small room inside one of the noisy barracks, with no privacy and no freedom. The revolving searchlights lit up the inside of our room throughout the night. Sleep brought no relief from the sense of helplessness and extreme boredom that soon permeated my life.

For days, weeks, and months on end, there was absolutely nothing to do. At first, I was too stunned to do anything. Even simple tasks were difficult. Later, I became depressed and angry. Even if I had wanted to, there really wasn't anything to do. When I wasn't lying on my cot in the boxy space we euphemistically called our "apartment," I wandered listlessly around the dusty roads crisscrossing the camp just to pass the time. There were many others—thousands of people—who did the same.

Back home, the Japanese were an industrious people who were always busy doing something constructive. Now, the rhythm of our daily lives was completely disrupted. Families didn't eat together anymore. Children started to hang out with their friends, disobeying their parents, and roaming the prison grounds, looking for trouble—looking for anything to relieve the boredom. The breakdown of the traditional family structure was ominous.

The community recognized this difficulty, so it wasn't long before concerned people began taking matters into their own hands. People started educational classes for children and adults. Others organized various sports leagues, and arts and crafts groups flourished. Some people pooled their small contributions to buy supplies in bulk and establish a canteen to provide some of the basic necessities for daily life. Radios were the new-fangled gadget of the time, so a class was created to explain how they worked. Yoneichi eagerly attended this class.

Early on, a bilingual camp newspaper sprang up, written and published by internees, and it immediately became the single most important community-building force in the concentration camp. Having a daily source of information was critical to our well-being, and it helped restore a sense of normalcy to our lives. One popular section was the schedule of all of the new activities going on. Movies were shown a couple of times a week for a small fee. People organized tournaments for baseball, Ping-Pong, and other games. There were dances, concerts, and beauty contests. Through our self-governance, community leaders emerged, a few of whom took their skills on to positions of national prominence after the war.

Out of thin air, in the middle of a barren wasteland, a community sprang up. With nothing but our own creativity, a few resources, and an abundance of time, people made things happen. The U.S. government did very little to provide activities for internees in the ten internment camps throughout the western United States. We had to figure it out for ourselves—motivated by our own boredom and resourcefulness—which provided the seeds for our creativity, progress, and growth as a people.

We were pulled from our scattered homes across four states and jammed into huge camps. We were diverse in terms of age, lifestyle, and our experiences with racism, and we didn't necessarily understand each other. But our common stresses did make us into a single community, however forced.

My own struggles in camp mirrored those of the larger Japanese-American community. After the initial shock of relocation wore off, I had to adapt to a routine not of my choosing, with little freedom, and no apparent future. My life seemed to hold no hope for anything besides the boring monotony of camp. For two years, my life was stuck in neutral. Out of my anger, confusion, and fear, I faced a choice: *Do I sink into bitterness, or do I make something out of my life in spite of my circumstances? And if so, how?*

From the beginning, my brother seemed to have an easier time in camp than I did. Yoneichi was two years older than me, and as a male, he was brought up to be outgoing and assertive. He made friends easily and participated in a wide variety of activities in camp—far more than I did.

As our imprisonment dragged on, simmering anger and conflicts within all of the camps became more evident. While I hated being in camp as much as anyone, it was still difficult for me to understand the fury some internees displayed over our situation. At the time, I did not know of the brutally harsh treatment that many Japanese Americans had suffered during their evacuations, far worse than I had experienced. Nor did I know of the prejudice they had faced for many years, especially in California.

Yoneichi bravely chose to enter the draft, like many Japanese Americans both inside the camps and throughout the United States and Hawaii. It was a surprisingly easy choice for him; at least, it seemed that way. It was much harder on Mama-san and me. In retrospect, I'm sure he talked about it at length with his friends, but he never let on.

In June 1944, when Yoneichi left camp for basic training in the Army, it was the first time we had been separated as a family for any length of time. It was right after D-Day, the huge invasion of Europe by the Allied forces, and the news from overseas was terrifying. We all knew, but didn't talk about, the obvious risk that we might never see him again. It was such a horrible thought that I couldn't stand it. When the bus took Yoneichi away, it felt like a piece of my heart left with him.

For several weeks after Yoneichi left, I wandered around the camp, looking but not seeing—I couldn't find an outlet for my anguish. I felt abandoned. I couldn't even talk to Mama-san, who was dealing with her own grief. What would I do without my older brother around? It was one of the hardest periods of my whole life.

I walked the roads of the camp endlessly, staring at the sagebrush and mountains beyond the barbed wire, oblivious to the armed guards that watched my every movement. All I had were my memories, but even those seemed vague and out of reach. Days dragged on, and each day was the same, with no relief in sight. It was just like all of the other boring days in camp, except for one thing: I could no longer rely upon my brother.

Ironically, the boredom of enforced idleness created the crisis that led me to my life's work. The cumulative stress of two years of captivity and the lack of meaning in my life had taken its toll. Yoneichi's departure created an even bigger void and finally lit the fuse. As I grappled with my distress, it slowly dawned on me—I needed to *do* something. *Anything.*

After a while, a thought occurred to me. I went to the administration building and made inquiries at the employment office. An opening for a nurse's aide at the camp hospital caught my eye.

This reminded me of a conversation I had had with Mama-san many years earlier. When I was still an infant, she was hospitalized with a ruptured appendix. "The nurses were so wonderful to me," she said. "They bathed me, fed me, took care of my personal needs, and made me as comfortable as they could. They never backed away from doing difficult or unpleasant tasks to help me recover."

Those nurses had saved my mother's life.

I decided to fill out an application. The receptionist asked me to wait and took my form to an inner office. The speed of the response surprised me. They wanted me to start right away! Suddenly, I was needed and valued.

The next day, I met the head nurse, a white woman whom I liked immediately. She gave me a nurse's aide uniform and took me under her wing. She introduced me to some of the staff, gave me a tour of the hospital, and instructed me on basic sanitation practices. She assigned me to some simple tasks, such as passing out fresh water and reading materials to the patients. On that first day, I could feel my future expanding before me.

For the first time in the concentration camps, I felt in control of my own destiny. I was part of a team that was doing important work. Once again, my life had meaning. I would later go on to nursing school and a career where I personally witnessed many exciting advances in the practice of medicine. Nursing gave my life purpose. I could become a team member, a healer, and a valued member of society. This decision, spawned from a sea of boredom, inspired me throughout my twenty-eight-year career as a registered nurse.

Boredom serves an important function. Whether we heed it or not, it is a signal that we need to make a change. A healthy response to boredom can transform a person's life—or even a whole community.

Young people need to experience a certain amount of unstructured time in order to find out who they are and what they want to become. Today's plugged-in world of nonstop stimulation may ultimately be unsatisfying because repeated distractions only postpone the inner journey of self-discovery that we all must make in order to lead fulfilling lives.

Hard work can be good for young people of sound body and can lead to personal growth. My children worked hard during the berry harvest at the family farm for years. I believe this helped them develop the patience, perseverance, and resourcefulness to eventually earn advanced degrees. Along the way, they also learned to be comfortable around people from all walks of life, working shoulder-to-shoulder with many others in the fields.

The boredom that faced the Japanese-American internees during the war brought the community together to create constructive activities in the camps. Many internees went on to achieve individual success after the war, becoming leaders in business, academia, and government, including several prominent members of Congress. Decades later, the Japanese-American community would once again come together, this time to insist on an official apology from the U.S. government for our wrongful imprisonment. In 1988, the U.S. government apologized to Japanese Americans for its wrongdoing. This was a hard fought civil rights victory. Now, the Japanese-American community continues to flourish decades, and generations, later.

A pivotal point in my own life journey happened in the most unlikely of places—a crowded, dusty camp surrounded by barbed wire. While I wouldn't wish incarceration and its accompanying boredom upon anyone, the experience of having to face myself, alone, and without distractions, had its merits. Instead of immersing myself in bitterness and resentment, and turning to destructive behaviors, I found my life's purpose, which has brought me great emotional and spiritual wealth.

Now in my elder years, I see that my boredom was a doorway, disguised as a barrier. I found the courage to open that door and walk through it to a new life.

CHAPTER FOUR

Do What Needs to Be Done with Gratitude

*M*ama-san had a way of quietly, yet powerfully, offering her words of wisdom—words that more often than not would stay with me for a lifetime. She regularly infused her days with gratitude, often acknowledging others, or the blessings of her life, or the beauty of a moment in nature. It was not uncommon to see Mama-san strolling through her garden, bending down to admire brilliant-faced flowers or vegetables hanging on vines like ornaments.

One summer night after dinner, Mama-san and I worked side-by-side, cleaning up the kitchen after a whirlwind of activity. We were hosting fifteen Japanese-American teenage boys who were temporarily living on the farm to help with the harvest. At the time, I was just fourteen years old. Methodically, Mama-san washed the mountain of dishes, and I dried them. Occasionally, we shared conversation, followed by silence. As she handed me the last plate, Mama-san looked at me and said, "We are fortunate to have Papa-san, who has always worked so hard for all of us, to provide what we need to live a good life."

She paused, then added, "And I am proud of you and Yoneichi-san for how you both do your best in everything you do."

After that, she dropped in one more comment without much emphasis, but I heard it. "As you live your life, observe what is going on around you. You might see something that no one else has noticed. Maybe there is something that needs to be done that no one else has thought of."

Mama-san looked over and caught my eye, then turned back to her work. "Try to anticipate what is needed, and then do it, without having to be asked or told."

That was all she said, but she had that enigmatic smile, her steady gaze that told me this was important. We finished cleaning the kitchen in silence as I thought about this idea.

In the days after our conversation, I started paying attention to her, and to my surroundings, in a new way. At first, I noticed simple things. I would see something missing from the dinner table, or some chore that needed to be done, and I just took care of it without being asked. Sometimes, Mama-san gave me a smile that told me she noticed, and was proud of me for paying attention to others. As a young teen, this kind of acknowledgment boosted my self-esteem and inspired me to do more.

I realized Mama-san had done things like this ever since I could remember, but now I came to appreciate how deliberate her actions were. When our family was working in the field, she would quietly disappear and return with a snack and a pitcher of cool water, just when we needed it the most. Other times, I would get drowsy while reading or doing schoolwork on the couch, and she would lay a blanket over me, allowing me to slide into a luxurious nap. Her thoughtfulness often made me wonder if she could read my mind. Now, I was beginning to understand why.

Eventually, looking for things that needed to be done became a way of life for me. I discovered it is an art form, a creative and fulfilling way to express myself. It's like reading between the lines or finding subtle clues in a puzzle.

At the time, I thought of Mama-san's advice as being merely a way to become even more polite and thoughtful, and I enjoyed how it brought me closer to other people. However, all of that changed a few short years later when, in 1942, my family was swept up in the Japanese-American internment experience. In the concentration camps, nothing we could do would free us from our barbed-wire prison, or from the hopelessness that pervaded our lives. At that point in my life, "do what needs to be done" seemed like a futile exercise.

But it was in this desolate, crowded camp in the middle of a desert that Mama-san's words of wisdom would reveal a far more profound meaning. With nothing but love and her own ingenuity, she figured out what needed to be done to save me from the crushing despair and anguish of the camps. The wisdom of this life philosophy revealed itself as Mama-san's greatest strength. In my darkest hours, she was at her very best.

With nothing else to do, especially in the first few months in the concentration camps, people complained constantly. They talked about the awful food, the stifling heat, the dust, the crowded conditions, the primitive housing, and a host of other problems—all perfectly legitimate complaints. And yet, I never heard either of my parents complain.

Mama-san was especially gracious, even in the face of imprisonment. She would listen attentively as other women described the deplorable conditions over and over.

"Yes, it is difficult, isn't it?" she would say. "I have those same concerns. All we can do now is hope that this will end soon and we can all go home."

Those familiar Japanese phrases, *shikata ganai*—"it can't be helped"—and *gaman shimasho*—"let us be patient"—were like mantras as Mama-san faced each day in interment, determined to do whatever needed to be done to survive this experience.

I was only seventeen years old when we were banned from our homes and our lives, and imprisoned. The shocking disruption to my life created an inner numbness that I responded to by walking the dusty roads of the camp aimlessly, or lying on my cot for hours, staring at the lone light bulb hanging from a wood beam in our room. There wasn't any reason to get up, except for unappetizing meals, which were served three times a day in giant mess halls. There was no school during the summer months, no household chores, no groceries to buy, no meals to prepare, and no job to occupy my time.

Fortunately, Mama-san kept a watchful eye on me. Even in the midst of a barren prison camp, she found a way to bring something into my life that I desperately needed: a daily routine that had a semblance of meaning. We had been in camp for several months, living in limbo, with no end in sight, when Mama-san offered me hope. One Saturday morning I lay on my cot, listless after having slept through breakfast again. Mama-san came into our cramped, 20-by-20-foot room and saw me awake.

"*Ohaio gozai masu* (Good morning), Mary-san," she said with an uplifting tone in her voice. "I have some interesting news to bring you. This morning, a lady I met said there is a rich supply of seashells about two blocks from here. There are shells everywhere. Would you like to go with me and see how many we can find?"

I didn't really want to go, but Mama-san was persuasive enough that I got up and got dressed. When we walked over to the area, I was surprised to find many other women and girls sifting through the sandy dirt, collecting delicate small shells. The concentration camp was located at Tule Lake in northern California, and thousands of years earlier the entire area had been a gigantic lake teeming with life.

Mama-san and I squatted down next to each other on the soft, bone-dry dirt. Immediately, I saw a number of shells, so small I would have missed them if I had remained standing. I scooped up a handful of dirt and stared in wonder at dozens of tiny, spiraled shells, some barely more than one-sixteenth-inch long.

"They're beautiful!" I exclaimed, open-mouthed.

"And look how small they are!" Mama-san replied, peering into my palms.

There must have been thousands of shells within arm's reach. I found some larger ones too, thumbnail-sized clamshells and half-inch long spiral snail shells, which were equally beautiful but far less numerous.

Mama-san and I stared in wonder at these perfect little jewels of nature. For the first time in months, I forgot about the fact that I was unjustly being held against my will in a concentration camp.

We began a regular routine, collecting shells for about an hour every morning before it got hot. After we were done, we washed and bleached the shells, and left them in the sun to dry. Later, we sorted the shells and stored them in jars. Soon, our collection grew, and we had to get larger jars.

The daily camp newspaper listed a wide variety of classes and activities offered at the camp. One particularly caught my attention: a class on how to use the shells in art projects. Mama-san and I signed up immediately. We learned to make necklaces, decorate brooches and pins, and create simple wall hangings. The instructor showed us how we could use fingernail polish and other kinds of paint to add color and variety to what we made. Before long, I had a collection of simple but beautiful homemade gifts that I sent back to my classmates and church friends on Vashon Island.

Mama-san's invitation to collect shells was the first of many interventions that began restoring a sense of normalcy to my life while we were imprisoned in the camps. Activities gave my days a certain amount of structure, provided an outlet for my creativity, and helped me to reconnect with friends back home. I would need every ounce of my new-found strength to get me through even greater difficulties that lay ahead.

Mama-san's inner strength gave her a sense of calm in many situations where others felt powerless. From her knowledge of history and her belief in God, she had faith that everything would eventually work out all right. These were the secrets to her optimism. In comforting others, including me, she rein-forced her own sense of strength and hope.

But even Mama-san had her limits. When my brother received his draft notice from the army in March 1944, Mama-san was devastated. I burst into tears and was inconsolable for days at the thought of Yoneichi going to war and dying.

I was young and inexperienced, and did not yet have my mother's wisdom, or even my brother's. With the war drag-ging on, prospects for our release from the camps seemed bleaker than ever. To make things worse, one day I overheard Papa-san and Yoneichi talk about a problem with our farm. Suddenly, I became aware that something was wrong back home. I began to fear that a crooked deputy sheriff might be putting our most prized possession—our farm—at risk. This was the final straw. I felt completely helpless, as if our future was already destroyed beyond repair.

One evening when we were all in our barrack, I burst into a hysterical fit of crying, not knowing or caring that dozens of people nearby could hear me. Everything seemed lost.

"I can't stand it anymore!" I yelled, slapping my thighs with my hands. "We're still prisoners! Yoneichi is going to die! We're going to lose our home and farm forever! Why? We haven't done anything wrong! There's nothing that can save us! Not even you, Mama-san!"

I wailed through my sobbing. Mama-san sat motionless a few feet away from me, eyes wide open in alarm. Papa-san and Yoneichi turned and stared at Mama-san, not knowing what to say or do. No one moved. In the long, stunned silence that followed, Mama-san realized the truth in my words. She saw that what was needed was a new perspective on our situation. She thought carefully as tears flowed down my cheeks. I sat with my hands over my face, unable to look at anyone through my grief.

Mama-san leaned closer to me. "You are not alone in your feelings, Mary-san," she said quietly, "because I have them, too."

"You do?" I gasped, looking at her in astonishment.

With the four of us gathered in the harsh light of our tiny room, she gently spoke to me. "There are times when things happen to us that we can't explain. We have no control. We are here because of forces outside of our family."

Then Mama-san moved next to me on my cot and tenderly put her arm across my shoulders. "We had no part in creating any of this, but we cannot expect to live in a world in which there is no pain or fear, where everything goes along without disturbing events. Our situation could be unbearable, unless we reconsider how we will face it."

She paused for a few moments and lifted her eyes upward, a serene expression on her face, searching for just the right words.

"Let's imagine," she continued, "that we are now twenty years into the future, looking back on our situation as it is right now." She looked at Yoneichi, then glanced briefly at Papa-san.

"Some of us *may* survive this time," she said, turning back to me. "Twenty years from now, we may have nothing more than the memories of how we conducted ourselves with dignity and courage during this difficult time."

Mama-san paused, and looked directly at me. "What kind of memories do we want to have *then* of how we faced these difficulties *now?*"

She dropped her arms and sat back, smiling and nodding at me. I blinked, dazed. *What an amazing question!* I thought.

Suddenly, I could see my present crisis as just one of many forces that would shape my life. This shift in perspective gave me the room to consider how I could survive imprisonment and thrive, even if the worst might happen.

With a single, startling suggestion, Mama-san transformed what had been a wretched situation into one that was filled with hope and possibility. Once again, she stepped up, identified what needed to be done, and did it! Thanks to her wisdom, I could breathe again, and finally imagine a future beyond the barbed wire that surrounded me. I also knew no one could take away the memories I had of my family's love and support.

Yoneichi's courageous decision to go into the Army got me to thinking about my own future. After he went off to basic training, my new job as a nurse's aide at the camp hospital inspired me to enroll in the U.S. Cadet Nurse Corps and possibly serve in the war. In the end, the war ended before I completed my training, but I had found my calling.

My career as a registered nurse spanned more than twenty-seven years and many different clinical settings. I spent many years learning the art of delivering good patient care while at the same time refining my clinical skills. Mama-san's advice to figure out what needs to be done served me well in the nursing field. I learned to meld both an intellectual understanding about a patient's condition and an intuitive sense about his or her well being. I developed a habit of ending patient care visits with a question such as, "Is there anything else I can do for you while I am here?"

In 1969, I was asked to be the assistant night supervisor of the Group Health Hospital in Seattle. My job was to ensure the smooth overnight operation of the hospital, including resolving staffing concerns, making rounds of all the floors to identify and address patient problems, and handling an array of miscellaneous tasks. One duty I hadn't anticipated was taking calls in the middle of the night from Group Health members with urgent health questions. One of the very first calls I received was typical. A young mother had a six-month-old baby who was having trouble breathing.

I asked the concerned mother a series of questions. "Did this come on all of a sudden? Does he have a high fever?"

She answered "no" to both. But when I asked whether the baby had a harsh or unusual sounding cough, she said, "Yes, that's what woke me up. And it's weird—it's almost like he's barking like a dog or something."

I asked her to put the telephone receiver in front of the baby's mouth so I could listen to his breathing. It was labored and noisy, but not so restricted that he sounded like he was strangling. It sounded like croup to me, a scary condition but not an emergency. I advised the mother to bundle her baby up and take him out into the cool, moist, night air to breathe. Or, she could sit with the baby in a steamy bathroom to inhale warm, moist air. I told her to call back if this advice did not help and to call her doctor in the morning.

This experience was greatly satisfying because I saved the mother an unnecessary nighttime trip to the hospital, and it also reduced the demand on our busy emergency room. Calls with emergency situations were even more important.

I remember speaking with one woman whose husband was experiencing chest pains. Back in those days, the general public knew very little about heart disease.

"He keeps rubbing his chest and his arm," she said. "And he just doesn't look good. But when I tell him that we ought to go to the hospital, he just gets mad at me."

After asking a few questions, I was convinced that he was having a heart attack. I had her call an ambulance as a way of sidestepping her husband's objections. Such calls not only saved lives, but they probably saved money as well, since early treatment is critical for heart conditions like this.

In 1970, when I was appointed the supervisor of the hospital's new emergency department, I recommended to the administrative manager that we needed a trained nurse to handle those calls, rather than transferring them to the busy night supervisor. The role would have to be based in the emergency department, where the physician on duty could ensure the accuracy of the advice given.

My proposal was accepted. I hired and trained the first nurse and the service began in November 1971. The program was so popular that it wasn't long before it became a 24-hour, seven-days-a-week service. Group Health members liked it because they could get confidential information on all kinds of personal health questions, without necessarily having to go to the clinic.

Today, this information is computerized and part of a sophisticated triage and recordkeeping system used throughout

Group Health. It makes the giving and sharing of information by all parts of our system efficient and accurate, while still preserving privacy and complying with federal confidentiality requirements. Patients can now email their primary care physician directly, as well as call and speak with a consulting nurse twenty-four hours a day. For the Group Health Cooperative system, the consulting nurse service saves lives, reduces costs, and improves customer satisfaction. For this reason, services like this are now in use across the country and even around the world.

The consulting nurse service provided a bridge across a gap that people didn't even know existed until the service became a reality. In my mind, I imagine Mama-san being quite pleased that her words of wisdom influenced me throughout my life, and now touch thousands of people's lives.

My mother had an uncanny ability to find solutions where no one else could. Her suggestion to consider what we wanted to remember twenty years from now about how we conducted ourselves today was her genius at its best.

I have come to appreciate that Mama-san's advice must have come from a place of gratitude. When I start with an appreciation for life, I see more clearly what needs to be done and I can choose whether or not to get involved. It requires all of my senses and an awareness of what is around me, and it challenges me to express myself in positive ways.

Mama-san's advice has remained central to me, creating a life that continues to surprise and delight me.

CHAPTER FIVE

The Pathway to Forgiveness

*W*hen I was growing up, one of my mother's acquaintances, Mrs. M., would make an occasional visit to our home—an event I always detested. As far as I was concerned, Mrs. M. was a self-important busybody who seemed to size up the Japanese girls on Vashon as potential marriage candidates.

"Ooooooh," she would say to one of the mothers in her loud, sugary-sweet voice. "Kayoko-san *certainly* is turning into a beautiful young woman, isn't she?"

Mrs. M. didn't seem to notice or care about the rest of us girls who could hear every word she said. One of the other ladies would always politely respond to keep the conversation going, but it was embarrassing. When she talked about me like that, I felt naked, judged, and violated. Her comments made me feel like a piece of meat, ready to be sold to the highest bidder.

But Mama-san was always polite with Mrs. M, as she was with everyone. Whenever I privately complained, Mama-san would say things like, "Now Mary-san, you know she only wants the best for people."

On one occasion when Mrs. M. arrived for a visit, I politely invited her into our kitchen, where she and Mama-san started a conversation that didn't interest me. By coincidence, Papa-san had a visitor in the living room, so I quietly withdrew to my bedroom to hide out.

When I heard Mrs. M. leave, I rejoined Mama-san. She looked up from washing the teacups and said, "Mrs. M. told me you did a wonderful job of receiving her into our home and someday you will make a wonderful wife for some *Nisei* man. I am pleased you did that so well."

Indignation rose within me as I listened to Mama-san, my face hot and flushed. I had considered my mother a role model for taking charge of her destiny and making her own choices, as she had done when she married my father and left Japan to live in the United States. For her day and age, this was a risky, unconventional route for a young Japanese woman.

In a loud voice I responded, "I will *not* marry a Japanese boy and live with him *and* his parents in *their* home!" I banged my fist on the table to emphasize my point.

Mama-san was startled at my unexpected outburst. "Shhh, Mary-san, we still have company here!" she whispered, gesturing with her hands.

"I don't care! And I don't care what Mrs. M. says. I'd rather be single instead of marrying a *Nisei* man and living with him and his folks!"

Mama-san looked down in embarrassment and didn't say anything more. I surprised even myself, and I knew I was being rude, but I meant what I said.

As I grew older, I realized the inherent difficulties of my position, yet I remained resolute on this. All of the *Nisei* boys I knew were nice enough but seemed boring. In high school, there was a white boy whom I liked, but I never allowed myself the luxury of daydreaming about the possibilities. Culturally, it was unacceptable. My parents never would have approved of my marrying a non-Japanese man. I was stuck in the middle reluctant to conform to tradition, yet uncertain of how to break free without hurting the ones I loved.

Some ten years later, I was living in Seattle and working the night shift as a registered nurse at Providence Hospital on the women's surgical unit. It was my first real job and I felt independent and self-reliant. Night duty was important, but lonely and usually dull. I craved social interaction with people my own age who shared my interests.

One day, I read about a group for college students called the Methodist Student Movement (MSM). While I was no longer a student, I wanted to reconnect with the Methodist church in Seattle, and this group looked like a good way for me to get involved again.

When I arrived at the church hall early for my first MSM meeting, I waited nervously while other people trickled in.

Finally, the meeting started and the youth director, Harlan, explained the goals of the group: We would fan out across the city and assist the pastors of various churches in their Sunday worship services, starting the following weekend. We would be given the topic of the sermon, and from that, we were to help organize and lead the service.

As intriguing as it sounded, I started to wonder what I was getting myself into. I was mildly panicked at the prospect of speaking in front of a roomful of strangers. I had never spoken in public before.

After reviewing a few more organizational details, Harlan read off all of our names as he divided us into pairs. Each pair was assigned to a different church and given the sermon topic. As we all stood up to break into assigned pairs, I found myself looking into the eyes of a man about my age who was smiling broadly and approaching me with his hand extended in greeting.

"Hi, I'm Chuck, Are you Mary?"

His handshake was firm and warm. We sat down side by side at an unoccupied table to talk, and I self-consciously edged my chair back just a little bit. This was my first meaningful encounter with a man in normal adult society, just a few years out from my time in Japanese-American concentration camps. As a teenager in the camps, I lived with thousands of other Japanese Americans under difficult circumstances. After leaving the camps, I led a sheltered life in an all-women's dormitory for three years while in nursing school.

My parents and older brother had always been protective of me. As I sat there that afternoon talking with Chuck, I couldn't help but think, *What would they think of me sitting so close to Chuck? It isn't proper for me to be so friendly with a white man!*

But quickly, I got caught up in our conversation and didn't worry much about my family's opinions. We had a job to do, and Chuck seemed to have a million ideas about how we could proceed.

"Here's one of my favorite readings, called God's Loving Kindness. We need to pick some hymns and Bible verses to use with that. There are a bunch of passages that would fit," he said, reciting one possibility after another from memory. His knowledge of the Bible was impressive.

Feeling pressure to hold up my end of the bargain, I leaned toward Chuck and said, "A beatitude in Matthew would go perfectly here, or we could use the parable of the Good Samaritan in Luke."

Soon, Chuck seemed to relax a little, and we had an enjoyable discussion about how we might work together during the service.

In my mind's eye, it just didn't seem plausible that Chuck was attracted to me—but clearly he was. His broad smile, eagerness to share his opinions, and his interest in hearing my opinions all said, Yes. I admired his gorgeous, dark, wavy hair and those beautiful brown eyes that looked deeply into mine. From time to time, I had to look away to break the intensity of his gaze.

Maybe he hasn't noticed that I'm not white, I thought.

As a teenager, the Japanese had been berated by white, male journalists reporting on the war. We had been imprisoned by a white male president of the United States, and intimidated by white male soldiers who guarded the concentration camps. When Chuck, a white man, was attracted to me, it seemed unreal. I kept telling myself, *He treats me like a regular person.*

Nothing like this had happened to me before. My parents never prepared me for this possibility! I looked around the room and everybody else was deeply involved in their own assignments. No one else was aware that my world was being turned upside down. As the meeting ended, Chuck and I confirmed our plans to meet later that week. I left the hall with my mind racing and a flutter in my heart.

Over the preceding few years, I had developed a deep sense of *haji,* or shame, as a result of the forced internment during World War II. Chuck was the first person who challenged me to reconsider this. I made several dear friends in nurses' training, and the support and acceptance of these Caucasian women was very important to me—but this was different. This was a white man. Chuck was my age and valued me as a friend, not as someone to be protected, nor looked down upon. After that first day when I met Chuck, I knew I would never be the same again.

Opportunities of all kinds opened up before me with MSM. With Harlan's help, I soon had a leadership role and met many people, some of whom became lifelong friends. After our first project, Chuck and I had relatively infrequent contact due to our busy schedules. He and I continued to work together occasionally, but mostly with other people involved. After the initial flush of excitement when I first met him, a slower pace felt comfortable and unpressured.

In 1949, at Harlan's urging, I went to Mexico for a summer work camp to serve a small Methodist church. When I returned, I enrolled at the College of Puget Sound (CPS) to begin my bachelor's degree. I chose CPS mostly to take classes from two esteemed instructors, and because Harlan recommended the program. By coincidence, it was also Chuck's last semester at CPS before he graduated.

To my amazement, Chuck started to seek me out at CPS, which I found exciting. As we spent more time together, I began to relax and really enjoy our conversations. Whenever we could, we went for walks. Each time we did, Chuck reached for my hand.

Our relationship deepened.

One day when we were sitting in the dorm talking, he leaned in close as though he wanted to kiss me. All I knew about kissing came from what I had seen in the movies. Scared, I put up my hands and said, "Chuck, I don't know how to kiss."

In the Japanese culture, I didn't see people kiss; we bowed to each other, caressed each other with tender words, and smiled a lot.

With a broad grin Chuck said, "It's easy and I'll be very glad to show you." He placed his hand under my chin and gently lifted my face. "Just relax."

As he came close, I instinctively closed my eyes and felt his warm, moist lips on mine. Electricity zinged through my body! Simultaneously, I was elated, scared, and shocked. I had to back away for a minute to catch my breath. Chuck just grinned as he took my hand.

"How was that?" he asked.

"It will take some getting used to," I said, flustered. Chuck nodded in understanding.

After that, whenever we'd go for walks, Chuck just held my hand and he didn't try to kiss me for a while. I felt more and more comfortable just being with him. Over time, I found myself thinking about him a great deal and realized I was falling in love! With Chuck, for the first time since the concentration camps, I felt equal.

During Thanksgiving break, we traveled to central Washington to visit his family. My family did not celebrate Thanksgiving, so it didn't seem important for me to inform my parents of this trip. Chuck's mother seemed open to our relationship, but his father, though cordial, was reserved. I later realized that Chuck's father was aloof and distant, even with Chuck. I also met several aunts who lived together in a nearby town. The oldest, Aunt Lena, was the one who seemed most open and friendly to me. She gave me a houseplant called String of Pearls, which I still have, some sixty years later.

Chuck graduated at the end of that term and left the campus to serve a church on the southwest coast of Washington State, several hours away. I saw him only a couple of times when he visited the campus, but he wrote to me weekly, long beautiful letters full of news and romance. One time, he sent Sonnets from the Portuguese, a famous collection of love sonnets by Elizabeth Barrett Browning.

At the end of the school year, I returned to Vashon Island to help my family with the summer strawberry harvest. In September 1950, Chuck concluded his student ministry and drove across the country to the Boston University School of Theology. With the two of us so far apart, our letters became even more important. He presented himself so beautifully through his writing that it almost seemed like we were sitting side by side. My imagination ran wild with thoughts of the life we might have together, untarnished by any of the sobering realities that daily life might bring.

By this time, I was enrolled at the University of Washington in Seattle. Both of us counted down the minutes until summer break. When he finally arrived in the lobby of my dorm, I rushed over and kissed him, not caring who saw us. We were almost inseparable after that passionate reunion, despite my full course load and part-time job at a nearby hospital.

A couple weeks after returning, Chuck took me out to a special restaurant for dinner. We lingered for hours, talking about everything and nothing. Suddenly, he looked nervous, something I had never seen in him before. He got down on one knee and said, "Mary, I love you so much. I want to be with you all the time. Will you marry me?"

Time stood still as his words echoed in my head. To accept his proposal would be an act of shocking disobedience in my culture. In 1951, interracial marriages were almost unheard of. At the time, I didn't know of any other *Niseis* who had married outside of the community.

Finally, I motioned to him to sit beside me. We looked into each others' eyes, hand-in-hand. "I love you, Chuck, and I do want to marry you, but this will be very hard for my family. My parents have always planned for me to marry a Japanese boy. That's the way it is done in my culture. They will be very upset. I will have to go home and talk to them about it first. I hope you understand."

Looking relieved, he replied, "Of course I do. By all means, go and talk to them. I'll be waiting to hear."

The following weekend I went to my folks' house on Vashon. I made small talk and helped out with chores like I usually did. At last, an opportunity came when Papa-san and Mama-san were in the kitchen together. I told them I had met someone, a *hakujin* (white person), in a church group.

"He's Methodist," I said, knowing that my parents were also Methodists. I hoped that this would make him seem more acceptable to them.

I talked about how Chuck was studying to become a minister and how I felt about him. Then I took a deep breath, and the words came tumbling out of my mouth. "I have received a proposal of marriage from him and I would like to accept it—but I wanted to talk to you first."

There was a long, dead silence. I couldn't look at their faces. Papa-san turned away and walked out of the house without saying a word or glancing up at me. As his footsteps died out in the distance, Mama-san sank into a chair at the table, weeping.

It was one of the few times I ever saw my mother cry. Through her tears, Mama-san said that I was bringing *haji* (shame) on our family. I was not surprised at their reactions, but I still felt devastated. Resolute in my decision, I was determined to maintain control of my emotions.

I watched Mama-san cry for a few minutes, but I couldn't think of anything to say that would help. With a heavy heart, I silently went upstairs to my old bedroom. I packed the few belongings I had brought with me and put them back into my small suitcase. My decision to marry Chuck was severing my relationship with my family, but I was willing to pay the price.

Mama-san didn't look up when I returned to the kitchen, my suitcase in hand. I chose my words carefully.

"Mama-san, I am very sorry to cause such disappointment to you and Papa-san. I didn't mean to do that, but I must go my own way. I hope you can forgive me someday."

My determination to follow my heart overcame any regret I felt over the loss of connection with my family. I looked around at the kitchen with its familiar round wooden table, four chairs, white walls, cheerful lime green cabinets, and polka dot curtains. Resigned to my fate, I left the house, never to live there again.

The ferry ride and bus ride back to Seattle were long and lonely, but I refused to cry. I didn't want to feel like a prisoner of war or a political refugee. I wanted to be like any other young woman finding a future for herself. With Chuck, I could just be a girl in love.

Fortunately, my roommate and I were very close. When I saw her, I burst into tears. Before long, she had me feeling better, soothing me with exciting possibilities. Together, we made hurried wedding plans, enlisting the help of her family and many others to book the chapel, arrange for flowers and refreshments, contact guests, and even make my dress. I felt an odd mixture of sadness, joy, and trepidation. Since I did not expect anyone from my family to show up, my roommate's father (whom I knew and liked) agreed to give me away during the ceremony.

We were married in the Wesley Foundation chapel next to the University of Washington on August 10, 1951. At the last minute, as the wedding processional was starting, Yoneichi appeared, wearing a dark suit. I was startled, delighted, and overwhelmed. Upon seeing my brother, my stand-in escort graciously joined the crowd of well-wishers.

Immediately, I knew what must have happened. My parents and Yoneichi talked it over and decided that this was the best way to handle the situation. It was their way of starting to bridge the gap. In many Japanese-American families, there would have been no contact whatsoever, so I was grateful for the gesture.

Yoneichi looked at me, smiled, and put out his arm. I took it and we slowly walked up the aisle where Chuck was waiting with his best man and the maid of honor.

When we arrived at the altar, I turned to Yoneichi and said, "Thank you for doing this for me. And thank the folks for me, too."

He looked into my eyes with an understanding smile on his face, nodded in acknowledgment, and stepped aside. While the minister officiated, I silently gave God and my family my heartfelt thanks for their generosity.

Not long after our wedding, Chuck and I left for Boston. As we drove away, I looked at the changing landscape and wept. I was leaving behind my unresolved conflicts with my family. I also left behind my plans for getting a bachelor's degree, which I would not complete for another twenty-nine years. I was excited by the idea of starting a new life with the man I loved, but I also felt oddly alone.

Today, it may be hard to understand how my actions could have caused such a stir, but at the time, racial boundaries in the United States were much different. It was rare and often shocking whenever cross-racial marriages of any type occurred, not just between Japanese and Caucasians. Many parents and family members disowned young people from my generation who crossed racial barriers to marry.

I like to believe that even in Mama-san's grief and disappointment, she believed there would be reconciliation in our family one day. She had the ability to foresee the future she wanted for us, and to act in ways that would bring it about.

According to the Japanese culture of that time, I had married beneath me, resulting in a drop in the status of my family. But for me, this marriage meant an essential elevation of my own self-esteem. What irony!

During those early months after our arrival in Boston, I took special care to write frequently to Mama-san, giving details of what Chuck and I were doing. Our lives in Boston were very different than they had been. Since she was always concerned about my health, I made sure to mention in my letters that we were both well. I described Chuck's involvement in school and my new job with the Visiting Nurse Association of Boston. In every letter I included my appreciation for my family and that I missed them.

It usually took me a good week to compose each letter. I had to think about what I wanted to write, translate it into Japanese, and then carefully write it out one character at a time. Then I sealed each letter and sent it off with a prayer that it might heal some broken and heavy hearts.

At first, I was greeted with silence, as I expected, but after about six months, Mama-san started writing back. She wrote about what they were doing on the farm, the weather, and various activities they were involved in with neighbors and other Japanese families. She never mentioned the conflict that we had experienced—maybe she recognized her own independent streak in me and admired it.

Chuck's graduation came all too soon, and we were one of several couples from Washington State who chose to return home. Two years had passed, and by this time my family's shock had worn off. They were getting used to the idea that Chuck and I were married. I anticipated the feeling of relief that all of us longed for.

When we got to Seattle, I found a telephone booth and called home. A pleasant, familiar voice greeted me. Since long distance calls were very expensive at the time, it was the first time Mama-san and I had spoken in over two years. We excitedly made plans for Chuck and me to visit the farm.

When we pulled into the driveway of the family farm, Mama-san saw us through the kitchen window and immediately came out to welcome us. Papa-san and Yoneichi greeted Chuck like a long lost friend. It was the first time Chuck had met my parents, and I was thrilled that everyone got along wonderfully, despite the language barrier. Once again, I felt totally accepted by my whole family. That night over dinner was a chance to get caught up on all that had happened since we had last seen each other.

As is typical for the Japanese culture, we did not talk about the conflict that had erupted two years before. There was an unspoken assumption that it was behind us, and talking about it was unnecessary. Our dinner conversation lasted long into the night.

About a year later, Chuck's status in the family was further strengthened when we arrived on the farm with the first grandchild, our daughter, Martha. Mama-san's eyes lit up as I passed the precious bundle over to her.

"*Haro, Masa!*" she exclaimed with delight.

She looked over at Papa-san, who was smiling broadly, and said, "*Kawai, desu ne?*" ("She's cute, isn't she?").

Yoneichi appeared from behind the barn and approached Chuck, smiling, his hand outstretched. "Chuck, great to see you again. How's the proud father doing?"

The two of them chatted comfortably with each other as they admired baby Martha's endearing features. For me, that moment crystallized my family's validation of my marriage, and any lingering sense of estrangement I might have felt was healed. It was more than enough for me to feel completely satisfied, but it wasn't enough for Mama-san. I didn't realize it at the time, but there was one more piece missing for her.

It wasn't until ten years later, days before the end of Mama-san's life, that she was finally able to directly apologize to me for her initial rejection of Chuck, and ask for my forgiveness. I was surprised, because from my point of view the issue had long since been resolved. But my acceptance of her apology allowed her to forgive herself and arrive at a place of closure.

I have wondered why she didn't raise this issue years earlier, while she was still healthy. Undoubtedly, she had thought about it ever since the incident happened, and lived with her regret. Whatever the reason, it was certainly a human and understandable shortcoming on her part to delay the discussion until she was near death.

Mama-san had her own path to walk toward opening her mind and heart, pushing past her generation's traditional ideas and cultural restrictions. Now, I see that in the parent-child relationship there are times when each can be the teacher to the other. Our children always offer opportunities to grow and expand and understand new worlds. Unknowingly, I made a life choice that offered Mama-san the opportunity to learn forgiveness, and to give it.

CHAPTER SIX

Reconciling Differences

An urgent pounding on our door woke my family with a start in the middle of the night. "Yoneichi! Yoneichi," a man yelled urgently.

There was more pounding. I sat up on my army cot, groggy and disoriented. *Where am I?* The searchlight swept across our barrack's window and I remembered—Tule Lake camp.

My brother leapt out of bed and opened the door. In burst Bobby, one of Yoneichi's classmates from Vashon. He was breathing hard, as if he had been running. "Ken Ishimoto got beat up."

Without saying a word, Yoneichi threw on some clothes, and the two of them ran off. My parents and I watched in alarm, afraid for Yoneichi and wary of the recent violence among the internees at the camps. The tension at Tule Lake had increased sharply a few weeks earlier. It was 1943 and the U.S. government had created a highly divisive Loyalty Oath that began to tear apart Japanese-American families, communities, and tens-of-thousands imprisoned in the concentration camps.

Around dawn, Yoneichi returned, grim-faced, his shirt stained with blood. We peppered him with questions.

"We took Ken to the hospital," Yoneichi explained. "His mother is going to stay with him there. He was pretty beat up, but he'll be okay."

"Does anyone know who attacked him?" asked Mama-san.

"No," said Yoneichi. "Ken didn't recognize them, but we're pretty sure they're from California, like most of the 'No No' guys."

As he changed his shirt, he continued, "Ken has been going around encouraging people to vote 'Yes Yes.' That's probably what got him in trouble."

Papa-san nodded in agreement. "At times like this, it is best to keep a low profile. The nail that sticks up gets hammered. We don't want to become a target."

"Yoneichi-san, please be careful," Mama-san pleaded.

I said nothing, but my stomach was in a knot all day. It was bad enough to be imprisoned and feel like the whole country was against us. Now, it felt like even my own people were turning on me.

For the first nine months of the internment, I was so disoriented by my new surroundings that I almost forgot that a war was raging. But inevitably, the war invaded our world at the concentration camps.

As the internment dragged on, simmering anger and conflicts within all of the camps heated up. While I hated being in camp as much as anyone, it was still difficult for me to understand the fury some internees displayed over our situation. At the time, I did not know of the brutally harsh treatment that many Japanese Americans had suffered during their forced evacuations, far worse than I had experienced, or of the prejudice they had faced for many years, especially in California.

In December 1942, a riot in California's Manzanar camp made it clear that something had to be done. Two internees died, and nine others were seriously injured. The concentration camp populations were dangerously polarizing into pro-American and anti-American groups. Among government officials, a consensus was building that these two groups needed to be separated to prevent further violence.

In a separate development, the U.S. Army announced in January 1943 that it was forming a combat team of young Japanese-American men. This, too, raised the question of loyalty. The Army clearly wanted only those Japanese Americans whom they could trust on the battlefield.

What followed was the government's infamous Loyalty Oath, one of the great tragedies of the Japanese-American internment—one that few outsiders knew about or ever understood. Each internee over the age of seventeen was required to fill out a questionnaire, which included two questions regarding our allegiance to the United States. There were two versions.

For men of draft age, the key questions read as follows:

Question 27. Are you willing to serve in the armed forces of the United States on combat duty, wherever ordered?

Question 28. Will you swear unqualified allegiance to the United States of America and faithfully defend the United States from any or all attack by foreign or domestic forces, and forswear any form of allegiance or obedience to the Japanese emperor, to any other foreign government, power or organization?

For women over the age of seventeen, and for *Isseis* of both sexes, their questionnaire was ambiguously entitled, "Application for Leave Clearance." The forms asked:

Question 27. If the opportunity presents itself, and you are found qualified, would you be willing to volunteer for the Army Nurse Corps or WAAC [Women's Army Auxiliary Corps]?

Question 28. Will you swear unqualified allegiance to the United States of America and forswear any form of alle-

giance or obedience to the Japanese
emperor, or any other foreign government, power or organization?

When the government distributed the forms, they immediately touched off frenzied discussions throughout all of the
camps. The questions were poorly worded, confusing, and
ominous, but we knew they were important.

For the *Isseis* in particular, the options were bewildering,
and the lack of information terrifying. Some speculated
that answering "yes" to these questions might result in their
"application for leave clearance" being granted, resulting in
families getting kicked out of the camps with nowhere to go
in a hostile country. But answering "no" could just as easily
mean getting deported to Japan in the middle of the war. For
the draft-age men, the choice was between risking death on
the battlefield or facing some other, unknown fate along with
their families.

The Loyalty Oath amplified the conflict that was already
tearing apart the Japanese-American community. Arguments
raged within families, between friends, and between groups
from the Pacific Northwest and California. Violence within
the camps increased, and continued even after the deadline
for turning in the questionnaires passed.

The majority of internees voted "Yes" believing that answering "Yes Yes" was the only way to prove their loyalty and earn
the respect of the wider community.

There were a number of legitimate reasons why people chose to vote "No" on the two loyalty questions. Some felt betrayed by the U.S. government that took away Japanese-Americans' basic rights, and wanted to vote "No No" in protest. For the older folks, the *Isseis*, who were denied United States citizenship, question 28 asked them to renounce their citizenship to Japan, leaving them without a country.

For draft-age men, it became even more complex. Traditionally, the eldest son in a Japanese family was responsible for taking care of his non-English speaking parents, so being "loyal" to the United States meant being disloyal to his family. Equally important, many could not accept having their sons drafted while the rest of the family lived in concentration camps, wrongfully imprisoned with no civil rights.

The young men who voted "No" became known as the "No No" boys, and were reviled by the majority of internees who voted "Yes Yes." The U.S. government punished the "No No" internees by corralling them into the Tule Lake camp for the duration of the war, where crowding was even worse than before and they had even fewer freedoms. Psychologically, those who voted "No No" were rejected twice—first, by the American public, and second, by the majority of the Japanese-American community. A few were imprisoned and fined for their beliefs. Many carried on legal battles in the U.S. Court system that lasted until well after the war. In the end, the internees who voted "No No" would carry this decision as a lifelong stigma.

In the camps, the Loyalty Oath put every family on the horns of a terrible dilemma. It was intended to separate the loyals from the disloyals, but it ended up separating Japanese Americans from one another for reasons that had nothing to do with loyalty. There were many other nuances to the debate. The uproar was unprecedented. Families were sometimes split apart, and for all of us, the anguish of this decision was unparalleled.

The Loyalty Oath changed everything for my family and me. Whereas my life seemed to hold no hope for anything besides the boring monotony of camp, Yoneichi's future suddenly came down to a single, agonizing decision—how to fill out the questionnaire. Yoneichi could have stayed in the camp, and many young men did just that, but he chose to enter the Army like many others both inside the camps and in the wider community. In the end, each member of our family voted "Yes Yes," although I must admit a part of me wanted to vote "No No," feeling betrayed as a U.S. citizen by my own government.

As a result of our "Yes Yes" vote, we left Tule Lake a few months later and moved to the Heart Mountain concentration camp in Wyoming. Despite my hope that the new place would be our "reward" for voting "Yes Yes," it looked almost exactly the same—dusty, barren, and isolated. But at least it was a change—and not so threatening. At this camp, the conflict was less overt, and there was less infighting among the Japanese Americans.

My brother left Heart Mountain in June 1944 to go into the Army. He eventually joined the all-*Nisei* 442nd Regimental

Combat Team, a legendary fighting force that, to this day, is the most decorated unit for its size in the history of the U.S. Armed Forces. Together with the 100th Battalion (comprised mostly of *Niseis* from Hawaii) and the Military Intelligence Service, which operated in the Pacific, the 442nd's contributions helped to significantly shorten the war. Their bravery also played a major role in changing attitudes at home toward the Japanese-American people.

Many Japanese Americans who voted "Yes Yes" condemned those who voted "No No." They would say, "You're not brave enough to go to war!" or, "You're leaving the fighting to others," or simply, "You're a coward."

The "No No" families were berated and shunned by their own people. Even as life gradually returned to normal in the years and decades afterward, there would be little or no forgiveness in the Japanese-American community for the "No Nos." The Loyalty Oath would haunt the Japanese-American community for decades—and still divides us today in the 21st century.

After the war, I gave little thought to the Loyalty Oath, preferring instead to ignore everything that had to do with the war years. My identity as a "Yes Yes" person became part of the unquestioned background of my life, a latent but protected aspect of my personality and my past.

Whenever I met another *Nisei* who was about my age I would ask them, "Were you in camp during the war?"

If they had been I would ask which one, and we would compare notes. But this was small talk, almost like discussing the weather. We didn't need to go into depth because we intuitively understood that the other person's experience was fundamentally like our own. But another reason was that we felt traumatized by, and perhaps ashamed of the experience. Who wants to talk about something like that?

For most of my adult life, nothing required me to think deeply about the Loyalty Oath or reexamine my position on it. It was safe for me to think of the "No Nos" as "those people." I was sure that no one I knew fit that description—but it turned out that I was wrong.

In 1991, just as I was getting used to my new life as a retiree, I embarked on what I thought would be an ordinary vacation. It turned out to be the start of a journey into my past, one that would force me to reevaluate the Loyalty Oath issue.

It began innocently enough as a road trip with my husband, our first in years, that included a visit to one of my childhood friends from Vashon who was living in California. While visiting, I learned that a mutual friend, Yoshio, was a "No No" boy. This revelation stunned me, but I managed to choke out a polite response when my friend told me.

"Wow, I didn't think anyone from Vashon was 'No No'!" I said. "But I guess it makes sense, given that Yoshio's parents voted 'No No' and he wanted to support his family."

Here was the first seed of doubt in the certainty of my beliefs, more than four decades after the war ended. This man wasn't bad; he was upholding a cultural value that made sense for his role as the only son in his family and as his parents' caretaker. Yoshio wasn't one of "them," he was one of us. Traditionally, the oldest son in a Japanese family is responsible for the parents, as they get older. By that rule, it was Yoshio's job to stay with his parents at Tule Lake regardless of whatever he would have wished for himself.

This was the beginning of the change in my understanding of the Japanese Americans who voted "No No." While I couldn't agree with Yoshio's decision, it still made sense to me.

For many years after the war, I protected my belief system by keeping the "No No" people at a distance—not just because I considered them "bad," but because the whole internment experience was bad. I didn't want to rethink my "Yes Yes" decision because I didn't want to think deeply about *anything* from that time of my life. Perhaps that is one of the gifts—and the challenges— of a long-lived life, the opportunity to re-evaluate and change long held beliefs.

In 1967, when my daughter Martha was in eighth grade, she did a report on the Japanese-American internment for a social studies assignment. She came home with a puzzled look on her face.

"My history book didn't say anything about the internment," she said. "So I went to the library. I couldn't find anything about it there, either. I even had the librarian help me." She looked right at me and scrunched up her face. "Did it really happen?" she asked.

It was as if our country had developed complete amnesia about this event. At that time, the mood of the country still had not yet fully recovered from the trauma of World War II, one of the most difficult times in our country's history. The costs of the war effort in casualty rates, economic hardship, and the physical and psychological toll on millions of veterans, were such that public sympathy toward Japanese Americans could not be tolerated until much later.

On top of that, Japanese Americans carried a sense of shame from our association with the enemy, and we were initially cowed into silence by fears of violence, both from the Caucasian community and from within our own ranks. We could not push for justice until the younger generations of *Niseis* and *Sanseis* (children of the *Niseis*) could see what had happened with different eyes.

That day when my daughter asked, I looked at her slightly surprised. "Oh yes, it really happened," I replied. "The next time we see Uncle Yoneichi, you can ask him; he'll tell you."

My daughter's questions eventually inspired me to write my story of internment. My goal was to convey to the next generation what the internment felt like. At the time, there was nothing in the literature that gave a first-person account that matched my experience. I wanted my children to understand not only what had happened to us, but also the emotional upheaval and self-rejection that I went through.

Inevitably, while doing research for my book, I learned of events that contributed to "No No" sentiments in the camps, especially the harsh treatment of the Japanese Americans that lived on Terminal Island near Los Angeles. I read an analysis of the Loyalty Oath issue, including the arguments on both sides, and I thought of my brother's friend Yoshio. But this research still felt intellectual and abstract.

As the manuscript of my book began to take shape, I realized I still didn't understand the "No No" position well enough to portray it fairly. Through a network of contacts, I found one "No No" person and attempted to reach out, but I was unsuccessful despite a promising initial discussion. I then reread the book, *Years of Infamy*, by Michi Weglyn. The arguments for the "No No" position started to make sense to me. This gave me enough insight to complete my manuscript. The wall within me was ready to come down.

Soon after the publication of my memoir, *Looking Like the Enemy*, I was on a book tour. One book reading in San Francisco became a life-changing event that felt like a trip to a far-off land.

California was home to the vast majority of the Japanese Americans who were uprooted by the internment, and during the war I had never really connected with any of "those people." Now, I wondered if I could finally make that connection—over a half-century later. By this time, I realized that I really needed to meet someone from the "No No" community if I was to continue speaking on the internment in an authoritative and balanced way.

When I arrived at the bookstore, a few people were already gathering, including an older Japanese couple who immediately captivated my attention.

"Hi, I'm Mary Matsuda Gruenewald," I said. "Thank you for coming to my reading!"

They seemed a bit shy and understandably surprised at my direct approach, but both of them were pleasant and attentive. They introduced themselves as Hiroshi and Sadako Kashiwagi. We chatted comfortably for a couple of minutes. They were active in the Japanese-American community in the Bay area, and had heard about my reading from a notice in the local Asian newspaper. Soon, I asked the inevitable question. "I suppose you were in the camps, too?"

They nodded, knowingly. "Which one?" I continued.

"We were both in Tule Lake," said Hiroshi, cryptically.

Ohmigosh, I thought, *Tule Lake—the code word. Could it be...?*

I nodded slowly. "Oh, Tule Lake. That must have been tough."

They exchanged glances with each other, then Hiroshi said, "We were "No Nos.""

There was a brief silence while they sat back and watched me. Inwardly, I was stunned and thrilled, but did not let on. I deeply admired their courage for revealing exactly who they were.

I extended my hand warmly to each of them, again. "That's fascinating," I said, looking directly into their eyes. "I am really glad to meet you both. Thank you very much for coming."

By the time the reading began, the room was packed, but the Kashiwagis were the only Japanese Americans in the group.

The presentation went well. I described my family, talked about the events leading up to the internment, and read several passages from my book. I made a point to mention the Loyalty Oath, although I didn't go into detail, knowing that Hiroshi and Sadako were there.

The audience participation session at the end was lively with a number of people asking some very thoughtful questions. After a few minutes, one woman asked, "Will you please say more about the Loyalty Oath?"

The question was so perfect that it felt planted. Without hesitation, I turned to my newfound friends. "Hiroshi and Sadako, would you like to take this opportunity to give us your views on this subject?" I smiled at them and gestured to the podium.

Without hesitation, Hiroshi got up and worked his way to the front of the room. He settled in front of the microphone and began speaking with the ease of someone accustomed to addressing a crowd.

Hiroshi described the Loyalty Oath questions and explained what they meant for the families who had to answer them. "We *Niseis* were citizens, but we were treated as enemy aliens.

And yet, we were asked if we would be loyal to a government that treated us this way.

"The government's questionnaire was essentially a contract. But a legitimate contract starts with a relationship between equals, based upon trust. That wasn't the case here. The questions were coercive, and the government didn't even have the right to ask those questions after what they had perpetrated upon our people."

He glanced over at me. I nodded back, encouraging him.

"For me," he continued, "My 'No No' response was a protest vote. I could not, in good conscience, simply pretend that the civil rights violations of the previous twelve months had not happened. I had to vote 'No No' to maintain my dignity as a human being. And I was willing to face whatever consequences that choice would bring."

Around the room, I could see nods of understanding. No one said a word.

Hiroshi gripped the sides of the lectern and heaved a sigh. "The Loyalty Oath took a heavy toll upon the Japanese-American community," he said, wearily. "A dark cloud came over us, turning friend against friend, brother against brother. Before, there was only one type of Japanese person. After the Loyalty Oath, there were two. And everyone knew which type you were."

His words hung in the air for a long time. He took a deep breath and looked over at me, standing to his side. I met his gaze, then turned to Sadako, sitting in the middle of the crowd. "Sadako," I asked, "is there anything you would like to add?"

She came up immediately, somber, and joined her husband at the podium. "The Loyalty Oath happened over sixty years ago," she said quietly, looking around the room, "but it still divides the Japanese-American community to this day. For those who were there, the feelings are just as strong now as they were in 1943."

By her side, Hiroshi nodded as she spoke. The crowd was mesmerized. I was hesitant to break the spell, for them as well as for myself. After this San Francisco reading, I could no longer think of the "No No" community as "those people."

The Kashiwagis and I continued to stay in touch afterward, and we developed a wonderful long-distance friendship. A few months later, I got a chance to meet their son, Soji Kashiwagi. His group, the Grateful Crane Ensemble, came to Seattle as featured performers for an Asian music festival. Soji is the group's producer.

After the performance, I found Soji backstage and introduced myself. He was expecting me, and already knew about the public encounter that I had had with his parents in San Francisco. Immediately, I connected with Soji, and he gave me the sense that he would be completely open and honest with me.

"I really appreciate what you did for my parents," he said. "That was the first time they have ever spoken publically about being 'No Nos.' It's been tough on them all these years, especially Dad."

"I think we all benefited," I responded. "I really did it for my own reasons, never anticipating that things would turn out as wonderfully as they have."

"But you made the effort," he replied. "That's what makes it so important. Most people in your position can't or won't do that."

Soji became quite solemn as he described a life-changing event his father experienced.

"It was in 1946, a few weeks after Tule Lake was closed, and life was starting to return to normal. Dad was back in his hometown, out for a walk. He saw a *Nisei* man he recognized approaching from the other direction. He was excited to see this man, and was ready to extend his hand in greeting. Suddenly, the man veered off and went up a side street instead."

Soji paused and looked down. "It was an obvious rebuff over their differences on the Loyalty Oath. From that moment on, my father felt like a pariah. He realized immediately that the 'No No' stigma would follow him for the rest of his life. And it has."

I was stunned to silence. I felt awful because I had participated in the judgment of the "No No" people. For most of my life, I had condemned them, too, without really understanding their position or how they felt.

While Soji talked, images and memories rushed through my mind. I realized it was time for me to act. "There is a pilgrimage to Tule Lake coming up this summer," I said quietly, in that moment unable to make eye contact with Soji. "I must go and make a public statement in support of the 'No No' people."

I lifted my gaze and was finally able to look at him again. "It is the least I can do, for your father and your mother, to make up for what I have done."

Soji lifted his eyebrows at this pronouncement. "That would be a courageous thing to do."

I thanked Soji for sharing so deeply and personally with me. We shook hands firmly, with many promises to stay in touch.

Though I knew it wouldn't be easy to publicly declare my support for the "No No" position, I was determined to keep my promise to Soji. Fortuitously, the focus of the 2006 Tule Lake pilgrimage was the Loyalty Oath. Two years before, I attended my first pilgrimage to a Japanese-American concentration camp, traveling to Minidoka; however, this was the first time I would return to Tule Lake since 1943. A few weeks after our discussion, I received the delightful news that not only Soji, but the entire Kashiwagi family would also make the pilgrimage to Tule Lake.

The main program was held on the beautiful campus of the Oregon Institute of Technology in Klamath Falls, Oregon, the town nearest the Tule Lake site. About 260 people of all ages participated, mostly Japanese, but also many non-Japanese people. We slept in dorms on campus. I kept hoping to run into the Kashiwagis, but it was such a big place with so much activity that it didn't happen until later.

On the second day of the conference, busses took attendees out to the site of the Tule Lake camp. The only thing that looked familiar was the barren landscape with Castle Rock in the background. None of the original buildings remained, although a few remnants had been restored, such as the stockade. Eventually, I found the spot my family called "home" for over a year, barrack number 7404 C, now, nothing but a dusty concrete slab.

I stood in the spot where I used to sleep on my uncomfortable army cot with searchlights illuminating the room every few seconds. I recalled the primitive bathrooms, the terrible food, the lack of privacy, the heat, the ferocious dust storms, and the relentless boredom of those years. The memory of the armed guards watching my every move behind barbed wire still made me shudder. Most of all, I thought about the terrible conflicts over the Loyalty Oath that had torn the community apart, and that had ultimately brought me back to this spot in an effort to heal myself.

The third and final day of the pilgrimage featured a small group activity—the moment I had been waiting for. I had volunteered to be a "resource person" for my group, as someone who had actually been interned at Tule Lake. I located our group facilitator, a Sansei woman, and arranged to be the last person to introduce myself.

This young woman, a granddaughter of Japanese immigrants, greeted me warmly and I placed myself immediately to her right. Soon, others joined us. To my surprise and delight, Sadako Kashiwagi arrived and took a seat, followed by Soji and his younger brother Hiroshi. The elder Hiroshi was not there because he was assigned to a different group as their resource person. I exchanged a quick but excited "hello" with each of them as the session began.

The facilitator started our group by having each of us introduce ourselves and say why we were in the group. As I had planned, I was last in line. When it was finally my turn, I launched right in with what I needed to say.

"I came to this pilgrimage because I am on a mission," I began. "I was interned at Tule Lake when I was seventeen years old. I have cried a lot of tears in order to work through that difficult part of my life, and last year I even published a memoir about that time. But despite all of this effort, I discovered quite recently that one more piece is missing for me."

I explained the Loyalty Oath and how complicated and terrifying it was for all of us internees.

"At first, I was so confused about how I should vote," I said. "I couldn't stand the thought of my brother going into the army to fight and probably to die. I knew that I had to vote 'Yes Yes,' but I felt forced into it. It was like giving in to the neighborhood bully. In the end, I realized my vote wasn't about loyalty to my country—it was really about my family being together. I voted 'Yes Yes.' Our solidarity would overcome any adversity."

My eyes swept around the circle, and I saw everyone looking back with rapt attention. I told them about the terrible day when my brother received his draft notice, and realized that on that quintessentially patriotic day, I could not have been anything but a "Yes Yes" person.

I settled back in my chair. "From that point on, I gave up trying to understand the other side. When there were acts of violence in camp, or threats, or protests, I dismissed all of the 'No Nos' as troublemakers who weren't worth the dignity of my attention. I told myself, 'No one that I know or care about would ever do such things.'"

I paused, gathering my thoughts. "And that's the way it stayed, for over fifty years. But when I started writing my memoir, I realized I had to know more about the Loyalty Oath. I read more about the 'No No' rationale, and it really opened my eyes. I had to admit, the 'No No' position made a lot of sense."

I glanced at the Kashiwagis, sitting in different parts of the circle. "But it still wasn't personal to me."

I looked down. "That's when I met Hiroshi and Sadako Kashiwagi. I knew the moment we met that these were talented, likeable, and admirable people. Here, at last, were real people who had voted 'No No'—and suffered terrible consequences."

I thought about Hiroshi being haunted by shame for all of those years after the war, and my eyes grew blurry.

"With my silence, I went along with the great majority of 'Yes Yes' people who ostracized the 'No No' people and made them feel unwelcome, unwanted, and un-American. I thought of them simply as 'those people,' whose viewpoint wasn't even worth understanding."

I took another deep breath. "I have come to realize that I have been wrong in my attitude toward those who answered 'No No' to the loyalty questions. I want to take responsibility for the pain I have caused them."

My voice started cracking as I continued. "And I want to apologize to Hiroshi, Sadako, and the Kashiwagi family for what I have done, and to ask them for their forgiveness."

Immediately, I broke down into uncontrollable weeping. For weeks, I had prepared for what I wanted to say, but I hadn't prepared myself for my surge of emotions. As the tears flowed, I gradually became aware that everyone else in the circle was crying, too. Several minutes passed as our collective tears fell and decades of pent-up tensions dissolved.

Gradually, my breathing returned to normal and I was able to look around again. I noticed that Soji was still convulsed with sobs.

Sadako was the one who finally broke the silence. "Living with the 'No No' stigma has been very hard on my husband, and on all of us in my family," she said quietly. "Mary, it took great courage for you to do what you just did. You have touched all of us here very deeply."

Several others echoed her remarks. I could see and feel the mood of the room relax, the tears and honesty of the inter-action absolving the past. Other people started comfortably sharing their experiences of the camps and the pilgrimage. I had the sense that people were reluctant to end the meeting, wanting to savor our closeness a little while longer.

Later that evening, I saw the elder Hiroshi. "I heard what took place in your group," he said. "And I want to thank you for having the courage to make such a strong statement. It means a lot to me and my family."

"I'm glad I had the opportunity to share my insight," I replied. "I could never have made that leap without you and your family to help me."

We smiled and slowly nodded to each other, an understated acknowledgment of our bond and friendship.

My journey toward reconciliation and healing was a long one, taking me more than sixty years. I had to start by reliving and working through the pain and humiliation that I experienced as a teenager in the concentration camps.

Then I had to take the time to rethink my beliefs. Although it seemed daunting at the time, afterward it didn't seem so difficult after all. I needed the courage to start the process, but the rewards of renewal, freedom from past hurts, and inner peace were worth it. Reconciliation opened up a future that I never expected, along with a close personal friendship with an entire "No No" family.

Reconciliation and healing would begin on a national level for the Japanese-American community in the 1970s after decades of silence. A grassroots effort took hold to confront the injustices of the internment. Activists demanded a formal apology and reparations from the U.S. government. Japanese Americans formed The Commission on Wartime Relocation and Internment of Civilians and began holding televised hearings across the country. Survivors of the internment testified about their experiences, bringing their stories to a shocked American public, many of whom knew little or nothing about the Japanese-American internment during World War II.

The movement culminated with President Ronald Reagan signing into law the Civil Liberties Act of 1988. Each surviving internee received a formal letter of apology, signed by the President, and a check for $20,000. While the money was mostly symbolic and could not begin to repay the losses we endured, many of us regarded this gesture as a profound victory.

This achievement would not have happened if it weren't for the sacrifices of the *Nisei* soldiers, like my brother, who fought so bravely during the war. And yet, ironically, the reparations movement was very much in the spirit of the "No No" position. The "No No" activists wouldn't be quiet, refused to go along with the status quo, and wouldn't accept the Japanese cultural perspective of shikata ga nai ("it can't be helped"). This was a different battle than World War II, but one that still needed to be fought to heal the Japanese-American community.

It took both sides to win.

CHAPTER SEVEN

Embracing the Self: Japan

The schoolyard was nothing more than a wide-open field, a blank stage for playing out our childhood dramas. It was well manicured, ready for whatever the new school year might bring. When the recess bell rang, I couldn't wait to join a group of my third grade classmates.

"Follow me!" said Beverly, as she leapfrogged over the first of a dozen small wooden posts. By the time the seven of us girls had leapt over all of the posts and turned around, we were breathless and giggly.

"Now, faster this time!" Beverly commanded, catching her breath as she started the return trip.

As I waited for my turn, I noticed a blond girl in our group watching me intently, an odd expression on her face. She was the one girl in the group I did not know very well. She must have been waiting for me to notice her. As our eyes met, my carefree laughter drained out of me.

Her eyes narrowed in contempt, her lips twisted, and she snarled, "You're a Jap!"

Then, she walked away triumphantly, her nose upturned, leaving me cold. All of the other girls stopped and stared, suddenly quiet. I had a hard time getting my breath. Shocked at the unexpected assault, I was confused and embarrassed. My ears burned in the awkward silence as I imagined my classmates seeing me in a new, unflattering way.

A Jap. Until that moment, I had no perception of being different from my classmates—I was just one of the group. But now, I felt self-conscious. In an instant, this third grader labeled me as inferior, not good enough.

At the time, I believed her—at least until I got home that afternoon. Mama-san was out in the yard, and as soon as she saw my distressed face, she knew something was terribly wrong. She listened carefully as I told her what happened, nodding in understanding and not interrupting.

When I finished, Mama-san gently wiped away my tears with her sleeve and assured me that this girl's mean words wouldn't really make a difference to my friends.

"Some people are like that. They say mean things, but what that girl did says more about her than it says about you."

Immediately, I felt better. For a minute or two, I stood there pondering what happened, then shrugged my shoulders and went into the house. As I left, Mama-san smiled at me, looking pleased. Although I was satisfied with her explanation, I never forgot the incident—not even some seventy-five years later.

Eight years after that childhood incident, my status as a "Jap" came back to haunt me—this time on a worldwide level. It was January 1942, and my junior year in high school was becoming increasingly stressful. The Japanese had bombed Pearl Harbor just a month earlier, and the United States entered World War II.

It was hard to concentrate on my writing assignments when the newspapers had frightening headlines nearly every day. Reports from around the world were not good, especially in the Pacific where Japan posted a quick series of military victories. In response to being at war with Japan, the U.S. government imposed travel restrictions, curfews, and other constraints on Japanese Americans living on the West Coast.

One afternoon at the school library I sat by myself, trying to focus on my work. After awhile, I put my pencil down and got up to browse the book collection for anything of interest.

A recent copy of *Time* magazine on the corner of an unoccupied table caught my eye. I thumbed through it, hoping to find something to take my mind off the war. Instead, I found myself transfixed by an anti-Japanese editorial cartoon. An evil, slant-eyed monster with hideous features looked back at me. It symbolized Japan's takeover of the South Pacific, as it victimized different countries and took innocent lives. The caricature had buckteeth and a crazed expression as it committed atrocities with cold efficiency.

I recoiled in horror. To my frightened seventeen- year-old self, it was my face, my features, and my straight black hair that were being demonized.

Is this how they see me? I wondered.

Blood rushed to my face as I looked around, embarrassed. Fortunately, no one was watching. I slunk back to my table, feeling exposed and vulnerable. My self-hatred started to kick in. There were times in the past when I had felt shame for being Japanese, but this was different. *Time* magazine was a powerful institution, read by millions of people. It was the mirror by which America saw itself. Now, that mirror was focused upon people like me, and there was nowhere to hide. I looked just like the enemy.

This was the first time I felt my country had turned against me. It would not be the last. Before long, any pride I had left was crushed when the U.S. government incarcerated my family, and my people. As the Japanese-American internment dragged on for months and years, with each successive frightening, demeaning experience, I subconsciously resolved to deny my own Japanese heritage.

For my own protection, but without consciously deciding to do so, I chose to become and act as white as possible. Over time, I merged into white society, adopted many white values, had many white friends, married a *hakujin* (a white man), and did not seek companionship in the Japanese-American community. This became the new norm of my life.

As an adult, I vowed that I would never go to Japan.

For one thing, Japan has not always been welcoming to its returning sons and daughters. In the years after World War II, Japanese Americans who returned to Japan were generally unwelcomed, mostly due to massive food shortages and severe economic hardship.

A *Nisei* colleague told me about his experience visiting Japan and feeling unwelcomed. Around 1980, he led a group of Caucasian physicians on a study group to Japan. He looked Japanese, but because he could not speak the language properly, the locals ridiculed him. When I heard this, I decided right then and there that I would never put myself in that situation.

But in 2004, I met a delightful, charismatic woman from Japan who changed my mind. I was on a pilgrimage to Minidoka concentration camp, the first time I had set foot in one of the camps in sixty years. Masako was one of the few attendees who was neither a camp survivor nor the relative of one. She was on the faculty of a small women's college near Tokyo. Masako was teaching in California as a visiting scholar, and had also attended an earlier pilgrimage at Tule Lake concentration camp.

We were having lunch together when I told Masako about my decision never to go to Japan. I expressed my concerns over facing ridicule because of my poor and outdated command of the Japanese language.

"That isn't a problem anymore," Masako protested. "It might have been twenty years ago, but not any longer. Japan has lots of signs in English now, and you can always find someone who speaks English well. Besides, you are missing so much by not going!"

I hesitated. "I have to admit it would be interesting to meet my cousin's son, a man named Muneaki Horie. Many years earlier my brother, Yoneichi, met him when he made a trip to Japan, but when Yoneichi died in 1985, the connection was lost. I have no idea how to find him."

Masako smiled broadly. "It's okay. You already have a friend in Japan! You can visit me when you come, and I will have some of my students help you locate your cousin."

Masako's generosity stunned me. It was a compelling invitation that I tucked away for future consideration.

In 2005, following the successful publication of my first book, *Looking Like the Enemy*, my publisher provided further incentive by suggesting a book tour in Japan. Fortunately, my publisher already had contacts in Japan, and soon I was corresponding with several people about the trip. Before long, I had a full itinerary, including speaking engagements in three different cities. As it turned out, one of my new contacts was able to locate my cousin Muneaki, and I made arrangements to meet with him and his family.

As I prepared for my first trip to Japan at eighty-one years old, I wondered what it would be like giving a book reading in Tokyo, one of the cultural centers of the world, and another one in Hiroshima, a city once devastated by the atomic bomb.

I wondered, *How would I react to these two very different places?* I also imagined meeting Muneaki and his family—the first time I would ever meet a relative from Japan.

In March 2006, I arrived in Osaka with my daughter, Martha, and my sister-in-law, Miyoko. The airport was an incredible blur of motion and noise. As we emerged from Customs, we entered a gigantic concourse with literally thousands of people yelling and waving, trying to find each other. I felt anxious and confused as I viewed the teeming hordes. I was a small cog in a very large machine.

Masako was right. Language was not a problem. Not only were signs printed in English, but sometimes they were easier to follow than many places in America that I have been. And many of the locals were eager to put us at ease and assure our comfort and safety. My awkward attempts to speak Japanese seemed to make the locals that much more willing to help out.

My book tour took me to readings in Osaka, Hiroshima, and four different places in Tokyo. In each city, I had at least one contact person, and meeting these people face-to-face for the first (or second) time was always a pleasure. These women gave generously of their time, energy, and oftentimes, money, in order to make sure that my visit was well organized and enjoyable.

I soon realized that the Japanese do most of their entertaining at restaurants, as each of my hosts found unique and wonderful places for us to dine together. These meals allowed us time for comfortable conversation in an intimate setting, and I got to know not only my hosts, but also their families and in some cases, many of their friends as well. We also strolled under the flowering cherry blossom trees, the sakura, resplendent with bright pink and white blossoms that came and went during my springtime visit.

Each of my book readings had a predictably Japanese sensibility. They were all formal, extremely well organized, and attended by well-informed people. I did not expect any of the attendees to have read my book, but as it turned out, many had. However, many Japanese were completely unaware of what had happened to Japanese Americans during the war, so my talk was quite revealing and informative to them. As a visiting author, I was treated as a celebrity and afforded many privileges. At times, I felt put on a pedestal, disconnected from the people who came to hear me speak. Even though I looked like everybody else, I still felt like the foreigner that I was.

One exception was at Tsuda College on the outskirts of Tokyo. It was a small, intimate school for women, and speaking before the students reminded me of many enjoyable readings I had done at home. My friend Masako-san was now President of the college. It had been two years since she first urged me to visit Japan. We greeted each other enthusiastically.

Perhaps the most moving stop on our trip was Hiroshima's Peace Memorial Park, now an international center committed to world peace, built on the ruins of the atomic blast. The Peace Flame, lit in 1964, burns continuously and will not be extinguished until all nuclear weapons worldwide are eliminated. I had been anticipating this for a long time, but I still wasn't prepared for what I saw.

Hiroshima was the first community on Earth to suffer the devastating effects of an atomic bomb. It has been rebuilt, and is once again a beautiful, vibrant city—yet, this thriving community will never forget what happened. When I rang the large Peace Bell near the Children's Peace Monument, its deep tone resonated through me and throughout the Memorial Park—one more call for peace. By ringing the Peace Bell, I joined thousands of others who had come to Hiroshima to witness the devastation of war and speak out for peace.

During World War II, I was appalled when I learned about the atomic bombing of Hiroshima, even though I knew it would bring, at last, an end to the war with Japan. Now, I stood at the site of the bombing—a mix of horror, relief, and sadness still churning inside me some sixty years later.

The following evening, I spoke to a group of educators at the Hiroshima Peace Park International Conference Center. Members of the audience were very interested in what the Japanese-American experience was during the war. I shared how stunned and devastated I felt when I first heard about the bombing of Hiroshima. I also read them a letter from my mother, who was born in Japan, and who still had relatives living in Japan when the United States dropped the atomic bomb—first on Hiroshima, and then on Nagasaki three days later. In the letter, Mama-san protested this action by her adopted, beloved country. It read in part:

In order to defeat Japan, America took the sky for herself and tried to crush little Japan. They had a bad bomb that shouldn't be used in the world and used it to try to make Japan disappear. With this in the history of the world, the big dishonor remains. For us here, we do not talk about it. We might try to hide it, but it cannot be hidden. This splendid America has done a very bad thing.

I let Mama-san's words ring in the silence that followed. No one moved. I looked out over the faces in the audience, seeing a few that looked old enough to have lived through the bombings of Hiroshima and Nagasaki.

"My mother was wise," I said. "She knew that we Japanese Americans were in no position to criticize our own government. But for those of you here tonight who lived through those two bombings, I want you to know that you were not alone in thinking that America had done a very bad thing."

After the talk, I stayed around to sign books and greet well-wishers. The first person in line was a well-dressed, older Japanese woman about my age, who greeted me warmly in perfect English.

"I know what it is like to feel that you cannot criticize your country," she said. "During the war, I felt ashamed and horrified by what Japan did in starting the war and causing so much suffering, both here in Japan and around the world. But when the bombs were dropped, I was torn. I sort of felt like we deserved it, and I understood that America had to do it in order to end the war. But like you, I knew it was an awful act, and opened up the possibility of even more unspeakable horror in the future."

She continued, "I am so glad I came today because you and I have something in common. Not only did I feel restrained from criticizing Japan, I felt like I couldn't criticize America either! For me to hear you say that people in America felt the same way as I did, it is like having a weight lifted off of my shoulders that I have been carrying for all these years."

At last, here was a hint of the connection to Japan that I was hoping for, and it arrived in a most unexpected way. For the first time, the Japanese people around me didn't seem quite so foreign. My heart began to open to them.

The most powerful, most moving experiences of my trip happened a few days later when I traveled to the Osaka area to meet my Japanese relatives. My Japanese friend, Yoshiko Koga, had helped locate my long lost cousin by sending a copy of *Looking Like the Enemy* to the local police chief, who knew everybody in the area. A photo of my parents in the book was the same photo my Japanese relatives had kept, some eighty years after my parents had sent it to them.

When the phone rang in our hotel room, the receptionist announced the arrival of Muneaki and his wife, Kayoko. This was the moment I had been waiting for. As I opened the door, a slim man greeted me with a pleasant, open expression on his face. We nodded at each other and bowed slowly and deeply.

"Mary-san," he said in English, smiling shyly, "It is my great honor to at last be in your presence."

"Muneaki-san, it is so nice to meet you after all these years," I responded. I felt an immediate kinship with him, the first blood relative I had ever met from Japan. I introduced my daughter and sister-in-law to them, and we went outside to begin our journey together.

Throughout our time with his family, Muneaki-san treated the three of us like royalty, all at his own expense. He hired a van with a driver for the entire day so that we could travel as a group. He hosted us at a wonderful, relaxing dinner with his family at a restaurant near his mother's home. We traveled to a famous Buddhist monastery at Koyasan, where we enjoyed tea, a fine vegetarian meal, a traditional public bath, and a restful night's sleep on comfortable futons.

The next day we traveled to Muneaki's mother's home in a rural, sparsely populated area of Japan, similar to rural areas in the U.S., except that the agricultural fields were generally smaller. The driver took us along winding, mountainous roads to the countryside where my mother grew up. We traveled past the Shimizu River, for which the area is named, with its crystal clear water flowing lazily along.

Soon, we came to the area where my mother played as a child and where her family grew rice and vegetables. We stopped and got out to explore and stretch our legs. I thought about Mama-san as a little girl, the youngest of ten children. She must have loved playing outside in this beautiful countryside under the watchful eye of her older brothers and sisters at this, her first home.

Muneaki-san pointed out two mountain ranges in the distance, one behind the other. "Over there," he said, "behind the second mountain range. That is where your father came from originally."

I was not expecting this revelation. Wistfully, I thought about my father growing up, wishing I knew more about his early years and his family life. A renewed sense of appreciation for Papa-san welled up in me as I surveyed his homeland.

A short drive further, we approached the town of Shimizu. Muneaki-san said, "Mary-san, my mother would like to invite the three of you into her home to meet her."

"That would be a great honor, Muneaki-san," I said, somewhat nervous and surprised, aware that in Japan it is not common for a stranger to be invited into someone's home. I thought to myself, *I wonder if I'll know what to say!*

We pulled up to a small but elegant gray house, which was similar to others in the neighborhood. As we got out of the van, my chest felt tense and I began to wonder if I could adequately converse with Shizuko-san. Before this trip, I had not spoken any Japanese since Mama-san died in 1965.

The yard was beautifully manicured. We approached the doorway and removed our shoes as we prepared to enter. I led the way to the door: still unsure of what I would say or do when I got there.

Shizuko-san had been waiting patiently for our arrival. She opened the door expectantly and met my eyes for a moment. "*Kon'nichiwa*," she said serenely, stepping back and inviting me in.

Her restrained joy radiated a desire to welcome me and make me feel at ease. Shizuko-san's short black hair was swept up away from her face, and at eighty-three years of age, she still possessed a natural beauty and quiet strength.

I placed my feet together on the *tatami* mat, my palms flat against my thighs, and bowed deeply. Words long forgotten and unspoken came effortlessly out of my mouth.

"*Hajime mashite o meni kakari masu. Kore kara, yoroshiku to onegai itashi masu.*" It meant, "My eyes are resting upon you for the first time. I ask for your indulgence from this time forward."

It was a greeting commonly used more than one hundred years ago during the Meiji era. People rarely speak such formal Japanese today. An image of Mama-san nodding her head and smiling broadly flashed before my eyes as I heard my voice sound just like hers. Mama-san used this greeting whenever she met someone for the first time.

For a moment, Shizuko-san and I gazed at each other in wonder. My words were obviously familiar to her, and she was as surprised as I was to hear them. She responded in like manner as we bowed deeply to each other.

"*Hajime mashite o meni kakari masu. Anata wa kangei watashi no ie ni iru.*" ("My eyes are resting upon you for the first time.

You are welcome into my home.")

Tears stung my eyes and a lump formed in my throat. We each took in the sight and the wonder of a newfound relative. In Shizuko-san, I recognized the same gentle wisdom my own mother possessed. I took a deep breath. In that moment, a part of me that had not felt welcomed in my own homeland was healed through an ancient bond of language and courtesy that is my heritage.

Long ago, when I was called a "Jap," I took that wound in, grappled with believing it—and history reinforced it. By going to Japan, I was really searching for my acceptance of who I am. More than anything or anyone else, Shizuko-san helped me find it. I had made the connection to my family of origin.

Now, I can say, "Yes, as a matter of fact, I am Japanese. And I'm proud of it."

After eighty-one years, I was home at last.

CHAPTER EIGHT

The Importance of Community

As a child, I learned that I was a "Jap"—someone "less than" the majority, which was white. When I was called this, I knew it was a way to put me down, to try to make me feel inferior. But it wasn't until Pearl Harbor that being Japanese became a major liability—a stigma.

During World War II, the American press and politicians demonized the Japanese. The media feeding frenzy helped to galvanize the public's support for the war against the enemy, Japan. But I was terrified by what this meant for me, and for my future. I was embarrassed to be Japanese.

It was a helpless feeling. Much as I wanted to, I couldn't change the color of my skin or the slant of my eyes. Newspapers, magazines, and radio reports portrayed the Japanese as evil supermen, bent on world domination. As a teenager, I learned to think of myself as bad and undesirable because I looked like the enemy. I wanted to apologize to people without even knowing what to apologize for. My very existence began to feel like one big mistake.

This stigma led to a lifetime journey of learning to accept and embrace myself, and my Japanese ancestry—to "undo" the racism from my early years. A trip to Mexico in my twenties influenced my self-identity in significant ways, helping me once again to feel what it is like to be accepted and welcomed by a whole community. It was my first step toward once again feeling like I belonged in America.

In the spring of 1949, the mood of the United States was optimistic with the country's healing from World War II well underway. I had been working as a registered nurse for nearly two years, living in Seattle. In my free time, I enjoyed participating in the Methodist Student Movement, a group for young people who wanted to get more involved with the church.

I was invited to participate in a summer-long work camp in Mexico. We would be joining Methodist missionary Miss Mamie Baird in her community church in Cortazar, about 200 miles northwest of Mexico City. Our job was to assist Miss Baird by doing whatever was needed to serve the congregation. My nursing skills would also be in high demand in Miss Baird's community outreach work.

I traveled with three others going on the trip, all young women at the University of Washington. Kay was working on a double major in home economics and journalism. Peggy and

Leona were working on music degrees. Peggy and Leona were blonde and fair skinned. Kay was a light-skinned brunette.

Peggy and I rode with her parents as far as San Francisco, and from there we traveled by Greyhound bus to Laredo, Texas. When we got to Laredo, we met up with Kay and Leona for the trip to Mexico City. While waiting in the bus terminal, Peggy and I went to the restroom. There was a sign above one door that read "White" and on the opposite side of the building was a sign that read "Colored." Being from the Pacific Northwest, this was the first time I had ever seen anything like that. Looking from one sign to the other, I was bewildered over which one I should use.

Am I white or am I colored? I wondered. *How strange, I have never faced such an odd choice before.*

Peggy saw the look on my face and took charge. "You're not colored enough," she said, confidently. "Come with me into the white one."

When we arrived in Mexico City, Miss Baird, a petite woman with flowing white hair, met us for a brief tour of the capital before the final leg of our trip. She was congenial, obviously comfortable with the Mexican culture after many years living there, and excited to have us join her for the summer.

When we arrived in Cortazar, we walked from the bus stop to Miss Baird's church. Along the way, the neighborhood boys' whistles and catcalls surprised us. The local girls didn't talk, but eyed us suspiciously. Miss Baird saw the alarm on our faces. When we got to the church, she explained that there had been some incidents in Mexico City involving students from the United States at the University of Mexico.

"The American boys thought they could date Mexican girls the same way they dated girls back home," she explained. "Unfortunately, that's not how things are done here, and the locals became very protective. Eventually, some fights broke out, creating bad feelings toward all American students, even here in Cortazar. I recommend that all of you stay on the grounds here at all times, unless I am there to escort you."

I was startled by her serious tone, and a little scared. In retrospect, I think it was more complex than that. Mexico is predominately Catholic, and in 1949 there were cultural norms that prescribed modesty in both dress and behavior for women. I believe my Caucasian companions were seen as flaunting their sexuality, simply because of their lighter skin, and Peggy and Leona's blonde hair. In addition, our casual American clothing was probably a shock to them. Even though our dress was conservative by American standards, it was different from the traditional clothing the locals wore.

The church building was relatively small and plain, but clean. Inside, it was painted a cheerful yellow, and it looked like an inviting place for people to gather. Later, I would realize how stark the contrast was between this humble place and the large Catholic cathedrals elsewhere in the area. It was difficult to watch destitute, malnourished people praying in cathedrals that had ornate statues and expansive gold-leafed murals.

The four of us stayed with Miss Baird in her home, and we quickly adapted to our new routine. A friendly maid named Luz cooked for us. She was quiet and efficient in the kitchen and I liked to practice my Spanish with her. In turn, Luz seemed to enjoy correcting my pronunciation and usage of common words.

During the week, there were several regularly scheduled women's groups and children's programs in the church. We saw the men only on weekends, since they were working most of the time. The first week was a bit confusing, but fun, and we just helped out where we could. We made a few clumsy efforts to use our newly learned Spanish phrases, which the locals really appreciated.

In our second week, Miss Baird and I visited the local hospital so I could observe the conditions there. I was struck by how bare the shelves were, and the lack of basic medical supplies that I was accustomed to seeing in the United States. It was disheartening to see how financially poor the whole community was.

Every Sunday, all four of us participated in the worship services to varying degrees. Peggy and Leona impressed everyone with their musical abilities. It was difficult for Kay and me to contribute much, since the programs were in Spanish, but we paid attention anyway, hoping to improve our language skills.

One day, a family asked Miss Baird if I could take care of their eighteen-year-old boy, Ascencion, who had pneumonia.

The family could not afford to take him to the hospital. I accompanied Miss Baird as she picked up and paid for the sulfa that the doctor had ordered. Sulfa drugs were the first widely available antibiotics, and I was familiar with their use through my nurse's training. When I met Ascencion's mother, she repeatedly said, "*Gracias, gracias senorita.*"

The family lived in a makeshift shelter that used tree branches for the sides of the house. In one corner of the room, Ascencion laid on a bed made from old pieces of lumber nailed together. A sturdy pole held up the outer corner of the bed. A worn, flimsy blanket was his only covering. The mother did her cooking over a small fire in another corner of the room. While they were desperately poor, I noticed that the dirt floor was neatly swept.

Ascencion was indeed very ill. I gave him the first dose of medication, and Miss Baird and I prepared to stay up throughout the night. The family had borrowed a kerosene lamp so I could observe him. The mother and the younger boys hovered in the background and occasionally whispered to each other, well into the night. Eventually, they all fell asleep.

I sat on a makeshift chair next to the bed and gave Ascencion more sulfa every four hours, along with plenty of water. In 1949, this medication was the latest medical breakthrough, and I had great confidence in its efficacy. I took his temperature regularly and gave him sponge baths to cool his body as his temperature soared. Shortly after midnight, he began perspiring profusely, signaling that the fever had broken.

Soon, Ascencion fell into a deep and restorative sleep as I held vigil throughout the remainder of the night.

In the morning, Ascencion's mother walked to the town square and returned with a basket of sweet rolls covered by a napkin. She started a fire and made café con leche for Miss Baird and me. I bathed Ascencion's face and upper body one last time, and then we were ready for breakfast. The mother removed the napkin from the basket and several black flies flew off the rolls. Miss Baird and I looked at each other and smiled as we each took a roll and ate them with gusto! We knew this family could ill afford to buy kerosene for the lamp, much less the sweet rolls for our breakfast. However, we wanted them to know we appreciated this extraordinary gesture. Meanwhile, we also prayed silently that we wouldn't get sick from the rolls, which we didn't!

Miss Baird's schedule was unpredictable. She would visit different members of her congregation every week, and check in with people who were having particular difficulties. Sometimes, all four of us young women would accompany Miss Baird, which was both fascinating and sobering to see how people lived in Cortazar.

Whenever we visited someone who was ill, it was usually just Miss Baird and I. I would bring along my little black bag, containing a few medical supplies, just in case. Occasionally, we visited someone in the hospital. When I observed the hospital's procedures, sometimes it was all I could do to stop myself from jumping in and taking over. It was painful to watch hospital staff make what I thought were mistakes or omissions, based upon the training I had received in the United States. But no hospital would allow a visitor to intervene in their procedures.

After being in Mexico a few weeks, I noticed a strange and different pattern in how the townspeople interacted with me. Some of them behaved much more openly toward me than toward my three co-workers. This was especially true with the Mexican women. While they were generally polite to all of us, they would speak directly to me and look right past my companions.

Coming out of the Japanese-American internment experience in which I felt less than other people, it was amazing and exhilarating to realize that the local people in Mexico held me in high regard.

Unlike the other three Americans, I felt comfortable walking around the town by myself. This was a startling role reversal for me. Confidently, I greeted locals with a friendly smile and wave. My Spanish was even worse than the townspeople's English, but we made do with pantomime and lots of smiles and laughter. I found myself having a great time on these walks.

My status as a nurse opened many doors for me. I represented a profession that was normally well beyond the locals' reach. Even for me to demonstrate caring was valuable to them, and they responded by welcoming me warmly. For them to actually receive medical treatment was an unimaginable luxury.

Miss Baird always went with me when we made house calls on sick people for the first time, but on follow-up visits I often went by myself. Miss Baird and I were always received as celebrities. Sometimes, there was very little I could do for the villagers, but they were still appreciative.

But I also realized that there was more to my status in the community than my being a nurse. As a darker skinned, dark haired person, I looked more like the locals than my three Caucasian friends did. For the first time in my life, I felt like I was a member of the dominant community. It was the first time since the internment that I felt at home in a public place.

During World War II, when I was in the Japanese-American concentration camps, I also blended in with everyone else, but we were a discredited, stigmatized group, imprisoned against our will. Being in Cortazar was nothing like that. There, I had a surprising sense of comfort and kinship with the community, and acknowledgment for what I had to offer.

Meanwhile, the other three women I traveled with found themselves in unknown territory. Most of the time they had pleasant encounters with the locals, but every so often they were greeted with jeering, name calling, and scornful laughter. Sometimes they felt threatened. All three came from relatively privileged backgrounds, and they had never been in this type of situation before. It was unnerving for them.

One evening, after yet another unpleasant incident, the four of us had a long discussion about the problem. It was obvious the special treatment I received was based, in part, upon my physical appearance.

Kay was aware that my looks had not always been an advantage for me. As a Seattle native, and as a college student, she knew about the evacuation and imprisonment of Japanese Americans during World War II. She had an idea of what I had endured during the war.

During our conversation, Kay looked over at me and asked, "Mary, you've had experiences like this in the past, haven't you? What was it like for you during the war, being Japanese?"

It wasn't the first time that anyone had ever asked me about this, but now I was unexpectedly cast in an honored role. I explained in detail what it was like to hear about the bombing of Pearl Harbor, to listen to politicians and newsmen denounce the aggression of the Japanese, to see frightening caricatures of Japanese soldiers preying upon innocent American citizens.

"I knew these were exaggerations," I said, "but I still couldn't shake myself out of my fear and shame. And of course, my fears ended up being justified. We were forced to leave our home, and we were locked away in internment camps for years.

"But some people still weren't satisfied. None of us Japanese Americans did anything wrong, but they didn't care. All they knew was that we looked like the people that started the war, and we became the targets for people's anger and outrage."

I described several incidents when I felt people's hostility firsthand, especially on the day we were evacuated. "When we got off the ferry in Seattle, there were men with guns lining the streets, yelling at us and threatening to shoot. Even though armed soldiers escorted us, I was really scared. Fortunately, it was a short walk to where we had to board the trains, so we didn't have to put up with it for long. That day was the first time I ever felt like my life was in danger, and there was nothing I could do about it."

My conversation with Peggy, Kay, and Leona was educational for all of us. Their disturbing interactions with townspeople helped them to understand what it was like to be part of a targeted minority. They got firsthand experience of prejudice directed at them for no apparent reason other than the way they looked.

For me, it was strange, but empowering, to find myself being the "favorite" of the locals. From the people of Cortazar, I got something that not even my own family could give me: a renewed sense of belonging to the larger community. When I was still a student on Vashon, I took for granted the feeling of connection I had with my classmates and neighbors. That sense of comfort was ripped from me by the trauma of the internment. It was the unexpected welcoming from the townspeople of Cortazar that restored something I didn't even realize I had lost.

From that point forward, I never lost that sense of connection again, even as my life's surroundings changed. My "community" would become whomever I was with, whether that was family, a new set of co-workers, neighbors in a new city, or even a gathering of perfect strangers.

I went to Cortazar with the intention of helping others, but I ended up with an unexpected gift—my self-confidence. I discovered that being rejected and imprisoned by my country said more about certain people in authority positions than it said about me, or my people. Ironically, I had to travel thousands of miles to another country to discover that I was an American, fully deserving of my place in the country where I was born.

CHAPTER NINE

A Good Death
Is Part of a Good Life

As a nurse, I experienced the death of many patients, some of whom I cared about deeply. I went through all of the usual emotions that one might expect, including sadness, regret, and perhaps relief if the patient had been suffering. Nurses have always had to learn to deal with both the emotional and practical aspects of death, and I was fortunate to have excellent support as a student nurse from the instructors and staff of the Jane Lamb Memorial Hospital in Clinton, Iowa.

My first experience with death was with an elderly woman who passed away while I was on duty. She was never conscious during her time on my unit, and she apparently did not have any family nearby since there were no visitors. Hers was an expected death. All of these factors made it easier for me emotionally—but not easy.

After she died, I was afraid, uncertain how to proceed as a nurse. I had never seen a dead body before. When my nursing arts teacher, Miss Schlapper, came to the bedside to help me, I was greatly relieved.

"Remember," she said as she stood beside me, both business-like and compassionate, "this person was special to someone even though you did not know her. We must treat her body respectfully. Let me help you care for her before you take her body to the morgue."

Then Miss Schlapper gave me instructions on the proper procedure to follow. We removed all of the tubes and other evidence of medical care, washed her body, combed her hair, and carefully closed her eyes, making her look as peaceful as possible. This dignified ritual was as much for the survivors as for the deceased, as much for the hospital staff and other witnesses as for family and friends. I would follow this procedure many times during my nursing career.

Because I witnessed many deaths as a nurse, this helped prepare me for Mama-san's final illness and death. Of all of the deaths that I witnessed, Mama-san's was the best and most profoundly satisfying for me. It was also a good death for my mother. In her final days, I knew how to make Mama-san as comfortable as possible. This was the least I could do after all she had done for me.

It was the summer of 1965, and she and Papa-san still lived and worked on the farm where I had grown up. The farm now belonged to Yoneichi and his wife, who were raising their family. My children and I were temporarily living on the farm that summer to help with the berry harvest, which was in full swing, so everyone had a job to do, including my three young children. Naturally, it fell upon me to take care of Mama-san as her health declined.

Besides providing her with food and water, I had to practically carry her to and from the bathroom. Daily, I changed the sheets on Mama-san's bed, rolling her gently to one side, then the other, as I had done for countless patients. I gave her sponge baths and massaged her tired joints regularly, and spent as much time with her as I could. I administered small doses of pain medication to make her feel more comfortable. All of this was sandwiched in between getting my children ready each morning to pick berries, and caring for their needs throughout the day.

As I did my best to ensure Mama-san's comfort, we reminisced about the past and speculated about the future. Late morning was our time together. Every day, we talked about long-lost friends, my childhood triumphs and tragedies, and recollections from her early life.

Mama-san was not afraid to die. She accepted and even welcomed her dying, seeing it as a transition to what lay beyond, and as relief from her physical suffering,

One evening in her final week, Mama-san slowly got out of bed and walked a few steps to her dresser. She picked up her simple gold wedding band from its box, and slipped it onto her emaciated finger. For a while, she looked at her ring, and then carefully returned it to the box. Mama-san looked content as she eased herself back into bed.

The next morning, Mama-san seemed especially energetic while I performed my usual care routine. As I finished, she stared off into the distance for a few minutes, a radiant smile spread across her face.

"Wherever I look I see God as a glowing white light, beckoning me down this long corridor to be with Him."

Then Mama-san focused her kindly gaze upon me as I stared back at her, wide-eyed. "I am impatient. I want to go as soon as I can."

She had a peaceful, joyous expression, as if she could hardly wait.

It was too much. I burst out weeping. Mama-san comforted me as best as she could for several minutes, until my crying ceased.

With one last effort, I asked her, "What if there was still hope? What if a cure for cancer were found tomorrow? Would you be willing to stay?"

"No," she said softly. "My work on earth is done. It is in the nature of this world to constantly renew itself. For that to happen, I must leave to make room for what will come after me."

Mama-san took my hand in hers and patted it. "It is time for you and your brother to lead now. You are ready."

She smiled and nodded at me. We looked at each other and held hands for a long time in silence.

In the time we had remaining, no topic was off limits, including Mama-san asking my forgiveness for her initial rejection of my marriage to Chuck. In those final conversations, no barriers impeded the coming together of our spirits. These were the most intimate, honest, and tender conversations I ever had with Mama-san. We both understood that it would soon end, forever.

Five days later, Mama-san died with a smile on her face and the peace that comes from knowing that any conflicts she may have had were put to rest before her death. In her wisdom, Mama-san made sure she had a good death.

Mama-san's death was relatively easy for me because the two of us didn't have many conflicts, and those we did have were resolved in Mama-san's final days. I know how lucky I am to have had this blessing. Mama-san demonstrated how satisfying one's own death can be for those who have arrived at a place of peace and acceptance. It is a gift to have the time to look back upon a life well-lived, to savor the friendships and laughter, and to feel a sense of joy in one's achievements— large or small. I now realize these are the potential rewards of old age.

I spent only a few weeks actively grieving for her, which may seem like a short amount of time, but my experience was that she never really left me. She was gone physically, but I could see her quiet smile and hear her gentle voice encouraging and supporting me in everything I did. Without realizing it, after Mama-san's death, I slowly accepted my new role as the matriarch of our family.

Over the years, I have learned that my conversation with Mama-san has not ended. She is still my mother, but now I hear her voice from within. It took me a long time to realize this. The form of the conversation changed from the physical to the metaphysical.

Even now, some forty-seven years later, she is so much a part of who I am that it feels like she is still alive. It is because of this ongoing connection with Mama-san that I now approach the end of my own life without fear.

Papa-san's death was more difficult. He had been the anchor of our family, the one whose vision and careful planning brought us prosperity. Mama-san had supported him all those years on the farm so he could be strong. After Mama-san died, he was very lonely. He continued to work by himself in the fields every day, never complaining—but when he lost his wife, he lost his way. He deteriorated slowly over a long period of time, becoming forgetful and occasionally wandering off. Five years after Mama-san's death, Papa-san passed away peacefully from dementia.

I know I do not want to die like Papa-san. Over the years, I have developed some very specific ideas about the end of my own life. I have a will, which I update periodically, and I have a Durable Power of Attorney for both finances and health care. I've made arrangements to donate my organs upon my death. I have paid for my cremation and funeral, and I have even planned my own memorial service. The biggest job for me was disposing of most of my belongings. Having outlived my husband, who died in 2001, it was a huge effort to sell our home and sell or discard most of its contents. Doing all of these things brought me an incredible sense of relief—and freedom. I won't be burdening my children with these responsibilities.

I have discussed my death at length with my children, because I want them to be prepared when it happens. My children clearly understand what I do not want. Modern medicine has many tools for temporarily postponing death. At eighty-eight, I do not want a longer life at the expense of quality, and I do not want my family to suffer if I have a lingering illness. Sooner or later, I will have to say goodbye, and I want to go out on a high note.

I am not opposed to sensible, cost-effective medical procedures where good outcomes are likely. In 2006 over a period of a couple of months, I had several brief, odd episodes where my heart was "galloping" inside of my chest. My first trip to the emergency room was inconclusive, but two months later during a second visit, the ER staff managed to record an episode on a heart monitor. My heart was beating in a wildly irregular manner, and one time even stopped for five seconds, causing a number of nurses to suddenly rush into my room. That evening, I had emergency surgery to install a pacemaker, which solved the problem. The whole experience was completely painless, and I never felt scared. Honestly, I even enjoyed being taken care of by a nursing friend that I knew from my days working at the Group Health Emergency Room!

My attitude toward medical treatment was somewhat different when I was younger. I wanted to live a good, long life, and my family needed me. If it had been necessary, I would have opted for things like CPR, dialysis, and other routine, life-extending procedures. But now, I do not want to be revived if my heart stops because there is probably no easier way to die. If I need dialysis, I will decline it because kidney failure quickly leads to loss of consciousness and a peaceful death. All my concerns and wishes are explicit in my Durable Power of Attorney for Health Care. This is my way of doing what I can ahead of time in order to have a good death.

From my perspective as an octogenarian, I believe healthcare dollars should be spent on the young and those in the productive years of their lives. In the United States, a large percentage of our healthcare costs are spent in the final days and weeks of a person's life. Of course, it makes sense to try to save a young person's life, but I don't believe that extraordinary measures to extend someone's life make sense for the elderly. Because of Mama-san, I learned I can peacefully let go when the time comes.

If I develop a lingering fatal illness, it is my intention to decide when I am no longer willing to suffer the effects of the disease. I will announce to my family and healthcare providers that I am ready to take the final step. At that point, I will reject food and water. However, I will accept comfort measures, such as help with moistening my mouth, caring for my skin, and providing pain relief, if needed. I expect that I will die within ten to fourteen days after beginning my fast. This is a simple, peaceful, and natural way to die. Fasting might not seem to be an appealing choice to someone who is healthy, but eating and elimination are not easy when the body is at an advanced stage of decline.

If I am ever in a position where I am unable to make the decision to end my life, due to dementia or being comatose, then I want my children to decide for me. I have already discussed this with them while I was of sound mind and body. They have my permission—and my expectation—that they will "pull the plug" when it is clear I no longer have any prospects for quality of life. My relationships with my children are such that I have full confidence in them, even to the point of ending my life.

It saddens me when younger people fight death in the elderly as if it were something to be avoided at all costs. None of us escapes death, and some seem to discount the suffering that can accompany disruptive medical interventions or a long illness. Death at an early age is always tragic, but at my age, dying gracefully can be a gift. It demonstrates how to accept the inevitable with humility and gratitude for the life I have been given. Mama-san taught me that the way to arrive at a place of contentment at the end of life, is to live one's life fully now.

Death is the way the world renews itself. It is almost time for me to leave and make room for what will come after me.

CHAPTER TEN

Leaving a Legacy: The Forever Forest

*M*y doctor had a serious, business-like expression on her face as she showed me images of my lungs. I could see the area at the base where they looked darker and different than the rest of the normal lung tissue. She asked a long series of questions and had me take several more simple tests. As a career nurse myself, I appreciated her precise and thorough approach, a blend of compassion and professionalism.

She paused for a moment to gather her thoughts, then looked directly at me. "You have a condition called 'idiopathic pulmonary fibrosis.' What this means is that a portion of your lungs is losing its ability to absorb oxygen, and this is likely to get worse over time."

I wasn't sure what she was going to say next, but I knew it would be okay, whatever it was. "Given the current condition of your lungs, there is a fifty percent chance that you may die within three years from this disease."

The doctor paused to give me time to absorb the news.

I knew I had become somewhat winded on my daily walks through the neighborhood. I assumed this was just a natural effect of aging, but now, the doctor's news neither surprised nor frightened me. At eighty-one years old, I had lived a good, long life already, and was somehow comforted knowing what my fate might be.

We discussed several different treatment options, most of which I refused. I had cared for patients who underwent these treatments and understood their drawbacks. For me, more treatment is not necessarily better treatment. I agreed to take a simple medication that would help me cough up mucous.

My mother lived to seventy-three, and Yoneichi only until sixty-two. I watched my father deteriorate into dementia until his death at ninety-three, and I knew I didn't want to go through that. As I left the clinic, I considered how I would bring this up with my three grown children.

Three years should be plenty of time to get my affairs in order, I told myself.

Shortly thereafter, I had a big headache on my hands. I owned a five-acre parcel of land on Vashon Island, which was taxed as farmland at a very low rate. However, the county informed me that I was at risk of losing that tax-favored status. For a piece of property that size to qualify as farmland, it had to earn a minimum dollar amount per acre, each year, and the value of our annual hay crop was dropping below that threshold. I read the letter from the county yet again, but it didn't help. I couldn't figure out what to do.

The county explained that I had several options to avoid having to pay a much higher tax rate. Among the other choices, I could rent out the property to someone who wanted to farm it, I could donate it to a charity, or I could plant it in native vegetation. The county rules were complicated. After not having thought about the land for years, suddenly, I was faced with having to make a big decision.

This was the same land my father had purchased in 1929, and that my family was indebted to for its decades of productivity. This land was my home when I was growing up, and it was the same land I had worried about so terribly during the war.

At the end of World War II when my brother, Yoneichi, returned from Europe, the land became his responsibility, and for decades he worked tirelessly to make the best use of it. As opportunities arose, he gradually expanded the farm, eventually owning fifty-two acres and two houses in the heart of Vashon Island. Each summer, he managed the harvest of the third largest berry farm on Vashon. He also taught at a Seattle high school, grading papers and tests as he rode the ferry between Vashon and Seattle each morning and evening.

When Yoneichi neared sixty years of age, and his daughters were grown and independent, he started preparing for his retirement. Eventually, he plowed under all of his remaining crops and planted hay. The land that my family was indebted to for so many years was at last allowed to rest, with only the annual hay harvest to keep the property in productive use.

Shortly before retiring, Yoneichi visited his in-laws in Vancouver, British Columbia. He returned with a bag full of acorns from their oak tree, which he planted in his garden. He must have thought that only a few would sprout, but he was wrong. Up popped an entire row of red oak trees, crowded shoulder-to-shoulder, threatening to become a solid wood wall in a few years' time.

At Thanksgiving dinner that year, Yoneichi chatted with my son David about his project. "Those acorns really surprised me," he laughed. "But I'm not sure that other trees would grow so easily."

When David asked if he was going to plant any more trees, Yoneichi replied, "I think it would be fun to visit the forests of the Midwest or the Eastern seaboard and gather seeds, and see if I could get some of those hardwoods to grow out here." With a smile, he called it his "150-year plan."

Less than a year after that conversation, my brother died suddenly from a heart attack. Before Yoneichi's death, he transplanted a single oak to its permanent location and dug out the remaining seedlings before they took over the vegetable garden. That oak tree is now twenty-five years old and twenty feet tall. It stands near a number of other much older and larger trees, including several majestic bigleaf maples, a cedar, and an ancient black walnut. But Yoneichi's vision, I am sure, was much grander.

As it turned out, Yoneichi's idea would be reborn. In 1970, when Papa-san died, I inherited half of my parents' original ten-acre farm. I was only forty-five years old. For many years, I gave this land little thought. It was always treated as just another part of Yoneichi's farm, for which I was paid a small rental fee.

But in 2006, the letter from the county arrived. What would I do with my property? With the recent diagnosis of my lung condition, suddenly, I felt like I was running out of time.

My youngest son, Ray, came up with a solution. One evening while I was having dinner with him and his life partner, Jim, he announced, "I have an idea about the farm."

I looked up from my plate with interest.

"I've always wanted to plant my own forest," Ray continued. "I read about it once when I was a kid, and I thought it would be really great to watch my own trees grow for the rest of my life. It would be a lot of work, and I don't know if it makes financial sense, but I'd like to give it a try. What do you think?"

As Ray spoke, my head filled with images of towering trees reaching for the sky, birds building nests in branches, and deer sleeping on the forest floor. This was my brother's dream of a family forest. I looked over at my son, now a middle-aged man. I couldn't have been prouder.

"Ray, that's a wonderful idea! Let's do it."

With the decision made, the reality of my damaged lungs began to fade into the background. I could already feel myself breathing easier. All the time my family was detained in the concentration camps, the thought of one day returning to our sacred land was what helped us keep going. Now, I could give back to the land that had provided for my family for all those years.

Ray sprang into action. He attended a three-month forestry class offered by the county. We wrote and submitted an official forest plan, which helped us retain certain tax benefits and a limited amount of funding for the project. Part of our agreement was that we would plant only trees native to the area, which was also Ray's preference. We located a source for tree seedlings, ordered some forestry supplies, and hired a surveyor to mark the boundaries of the property. Finally, we found a man who could plow the land for us, making it much easier to plant the trees.

Several experts recommended planting the trees in rows, ten feet apart, rather than a more natural-looking random pattern. This proved to be a wise choice because the grass between the trees needed to be mowed periodically, which was much easier with the trees in a regular grid. Mowing the grass conserves moisture and discourages rodents that can damage young trees.

We began our reforestation project on a gray, but comfortable November day. When we arrived, the freshly plowed field was inspiring. "Wow!" Ray said, as he surveyed the land. "Look at how beautifully it was tilled. You can't even tell that it used to be grass!"

The sod was finely disked, and the dark rich soil was smooth and even on the gently rolling terrain. The soil smelled moist and slightly sweet.

Ray brought a spool of twine that he had previously marked in ten-foot sections with knots and pieces of pink surveyor's ribbon. We started at the northeast corner of the property. Ray found the surveyor's mark, carefully measured in a few feet from the corner, and put in a single bamboo stake. Jim held the end of the twine at that mark while Ray unrolled the spool halfway across the northern boundary of the plot. When he reached the end, the two of them pulled it tight, while I stood in the middle and helped line it up. We laid the twine down on the soil.

"OK, that looks good," Ray called out. "Let's get some stakes and put them in wherever there's a ribbon."

After doing so, we carefully walked the whole length of twine along the remaining length of the northern boundary to the west end of the field and repeated the process. We formed a row of bamboo stakes 660 feet long.

We marked the whole southern boundary in the same way, giving us the endpoints of the rows, each 330 feet long. Ray and Jim rolled up the twine and unrolled it again, this time in a north and south direction. Starting on the eastern edge, we put stakes in every ten feet, wherever there was a ribbon on the twine. Then we flopped the twine over ten feet for the next row, lined it up, and repeated the process, eventually developing a nice rhythm. We made a great team. The guys were patient with me whenever I needed to take breaks to catch my breath.

Toward the end of the day, while I rested, I watched a carefully measured pattern unfold on that rich, newly tilled land. Just the sight of it gave me hope and strength. It reminded me of the time in 1942 when my family was at Heart Mountain concentration camp in Wyoming. Before Yoneichi left for the war, Mama-san carefully plotted to make a *senninbari* for him to take into battle.

It was the height of the war, and I was worried about losing my only brother. Of all the hard times we had in the concentration camps, none was worse than having to send Yoneichi off to fight, and possibly to die. My fear and hopelessness had begun to consume me. That was when Mama-san began to make a *senninbari*, a thousand-stitch belt, for Yoneichi.

Almost seventy years later, I remember so clearly that day when Mama-san began marking a series of tiny dots on a small piece of white cloth. She precisely measured the distance from one dot to the next dot with a ruler.

"Yoneichi-san is doing a very brave thing," she explained in Japanese as she worked. "We must do our part to provide him with encouragement and ho-pu (hope). From a long time ago, women in Japan have sent their men into battle with protections from the *senninbari*."

Mama-san was silent for several minutes as she completed more rows, and then she turned to me with a serious look.

"You and I, we together cannot make this for Yoneichi by ourselves. The *senninbari* can only be protecting him if we get help from a thousand women and girls to make our knots in this little cloth. They must all pray for Yoneichi to return safely from the war. That is the only way we can protect him from the bullets of the enemy."

Outside the window, I could see a constant stream of people walking past our tiny, primitive room—all Japanese Americans imprisoned in this camp. It would not be difficult to find one thousand women to help us out.

When Mama-san finished, there were twenty rows of fifty dots each, making a total of a thousand dots. Then, she fitted an embroidery hoop over the fabric and cut off a length of black thread, which she poked through the eye of a sewing needle. I watched as she knotted the opposite end of the thread. As if in prayer, she silently chose a dot in the corner of the fabric and inserted the needle from below, pulling it tight. Mama-san made a tiny, perfect French knot by laying the needle next to the dot, wrapping the thread three times around the needle, inserting the needle back through the fabric, and pulling the thread tight.

When she was done, she looked up at me and held out the fabric with the needle and thread still attached. "Now it is your turn."

After I tearfully made my stitch, Mama-san and I made the rounds among the girls and women of the camp, many of whom shared our plight. It took about a week and a half to complete. As we explained our mission, it was comforting to see nods of recognition in the Japanese women we spoke with. I felt connected to my heritage through this ancient ritual of caring and community.

Once we had a thousand stitches, we gave the *senninbari* to Yoneichi to keep and wear. I have often wondered about the hope and love and comfort the *senninbari* gave to him in his darkest hours, fighting in some of the fiercest battles in Italy.

We were fortunate. Not only did Yoneichi survive the war uninjured, but our land was waiting for us when my parents were released from the Japanese-American concentration camps after the war.

When Ray, Jim and I finished plotting the five acres for planting the trees, we stepped back to admire our work. The property was now a sea of evenly-spaced bamboo stakes covering the fabric of the land.

Ray had a look of satisfaction on his face. "I like it already!"

I smiled, knowing Yoneichi would have been pleased that we had begun to fulfill the dream of his "150-year plan."

Over the next two weeks, Ray returned to do some additional marking to indicate where to plant each kind of tree. At last, we were ready.

On planting day, December 27, 2006, I found myself standing ankle-deep in mud, huffing and puffing as I tried to dig a hole for a seedling. My three grown children led an eager group of volunteers, including the families of my four nieces and a large contingent from Jim's extended family. Because it had been an especially rainy winter, we all found ourselves struggling to find places dry enough to plant trees.

I tramped through the mud in my rubber boots to where we had set up a small canopy to provide a little bit of shelter. Inside were coffee, doughnuts, homemade soup, and hearty sandwiches piled on plates. Throughout the day we provided many other snacks to keep the workers fueled.

A number of long, brown bags lay on the ground nearby. Each contained 200 bare-root seedlings, waiting to be planted. More than 150 potted trees were grouped by species. We began planting Douglas-firs, cedars, hemlocks, and smaller quantities of a variety of deciduous trees native to the Pacific Northwest. Ray circulated among the different groups of workers, giving advice and instructions, reminding me very much of Yoneichi.

Despite the mud, planting day was a success with more than one thousand trees planted under difficult conditions. The weather was much better for a second work party a few weeks later when we filled in the majority of the remaining spots. We waited until early spring to plant the alders, as recommended by the professional foresters, because young alders are vulnerable to frost damage.

The final holes in the grid were filled in at various times. Some tree species were harder to find and we planted those the following year. Inevitably, some trees died in each of the first few years and had to be replanted. As the trees have gotten more established, Ray has started planting native shrubs, hoping they will eventually fill in to make for a more complete ecosystem.

Eventually, we planted more than twenty-five different species. Most of the trees are long-lived conifers, which to me look prettier than any fully-decorated Christmas tree. The maples and cottonwoods are deciduous and grow fast. The slower growing and somewhat rare Garry Oak trees have a special place on the southern edge, where they will get the sunlight they need to survive.

Whenever I get the chance, I walk through the growing forest, noticing the changes that happen from year to year. Although a few of the recently planted trees are still only knee-high, each year more and more of them tower over me. When they get as tall as me, I tell myself they have "made it," that they are guaranteed to reach maturity and live on for many generations.

I take great comfort in knowing that these trees will be here, growing strongly, long after I am gone. Ray showed me an alder that was the very first tree to produce its own seed.

"To me, this isn't really a forest yet,' he said. "It will be a real forest when there is enough shade that the grass dies out, and new trees start growing from seed on the forest floor."

Perhaps this will happen in Ray's lifetime.

To our surprise, one type of tree is already reproducing. We have found over a dozen "wild" seedlings of the beautiful Pacific Madrone, a berry-producing tree, apparently started from seeds the birds brought in from nearby mature trees. Like my family, the forest has not forgotten how to recreate itself.

Three years after we began planting, I saw my doctor for my semi-annual checkup. She scanned through the test results displayed on her computer monitor, and spent a little longer reviewing one screen. Then she got out her stethoscope and asked me to turn around so she could listen to my lungs. I could feel the round disk on my back as she moved it, repeatedly telling me, "Take a deep breath. Again...again...."

She folded the stethoscope and put it back into her pocket. Then she raised one of her eyebrows, giving her an amused expression. "Well, your condition has stabilized," she said with a slight smile. "Your test results show little or no change over the past three years. And your pulmonary function test actually shows slight improvement compared to last time."

Relieved, I smiled to myself. The doctor had confirmed what I already knew intuitively—at eight-four years old, I was doing well!

"I don't think I need to see you again for another year, but you can always call me if you notice anything unusual."

I had used the three years I was given wisely, and now the future held continued good health and my legacy. In my will, I arranged to have my five acres of land pass on to my son, Ray, who will ultimately deed the land over to the Vashon-Maury Island Land Trust, along with a sizeable donation to ensure that the forest can be maintained in perpetuity.

The property cannot easily be seen from any road, and few will ever visit the trees, but the wildlife knows a forest is growing, and it really belongs to them. A doe recently raised a fawn on the property. A variety of forest songbirds are moving in, awaiting the day when the trees are large and dense enough to support their nests in safety.

In August 2010, Ray and I visited the forest to do some routine maintenance. I was eighty-five at the time, my breathing still strong. A *Sansei* friend joined us. Linda was very interested in my forest project, and she also wanted to see the home where I grew up. As we walked up and down the rows, looking for blackberry plants and other invasive weeds, Ray provided a running commentary on the trees and gave a history of the project. Linda was suitably impressed.

"This is amazing," she said, surveying the scene. "It must have taken an incredible amount of work to make this happen."

"It did," Ray said, stopping to stake up a leaning pine seedling, "but the great thing about trees is, once they get started, the plant does most of the work."

It was a hot day, and Linda and I shared a bottle of water while Ray dug out a small, invasive Scotch broom that had survived earlier mowing. As he finished, he looked past me and pointed at something.

"Hey, look at that. We're being watched."

I turned and looked at a small, brown bird hopping toward us through the grass, only a couple of feet away.

"I noticed it about thirty seconds ago," Ray said. "Linda, for a moment, I thought you were going to step on it, but it got out of the way."

We watched the bird for several minutes, marveling at how tame she was. The bird fluttered up into a nearby tree, less than five feet away, clearly watching the three of us.

"I wonder if the bird is attracted to my water," I mused aloud, my bottle of water shimmering in the August sunlight. I opened the bottle, poured some water into the cap, and slowly reached forward.

The bird hopped down from the branch toward my outstretched hand, leaned forward, and took three long sips of water. I could scarcely breathe, in disbelief with what was happening. My companions gasped in amazement behind me.

I expected the bird to fly off, but instead she flew to the ground and came even closer. She hopped among us for several minutes, allowing Linda to take pictures. Later, we were able to identify the songbird as a Pine Siskin, a type of nomadic finch.

Ray stepped back from the hole left by the weed he had dug up. Immediately, the bird hopped over and ate several small worms that had been exposed.

"Well, how about that?" he said, leaning on his shovel. "No wonder she's hanging around. I didn't realize we were providing free dinner and drinks."

The bird continued to act more like a pet than a wild animal. We moved slowly so as not to startle or step on her. After awhile, it was time to move on. We were almost done with our work, and it was getting late. But as we proceeded, the bird continued to follow us, disappearing and reappearing as she flew from tree to tree.

We worked our way down a gentle slope to the last few rows where the tallest trees stood. Here, the soil had the most moisture of anywhere on the property, and the trees grew the fastest. We stopped in front of a fir with its elegant, dark green branches, its tips highlighted with lighter, neon-green, new growth.

"I love all of the native trees, but this is probably my favorite," Ray commented. "This is the largest and most beautiful grand fir on the property."

He reached in and plucked a few needles from the center of the tree. "Try this." He crushed the needles with his fingertips and held them to his nose.

Linda and I did likewise. I inhaled deeply the wonderful, pine-scented, fruity aroma. In that moment, the tree gave me the gift of contentment.

Linda smiled broadly. "It smells just like Christmas. Wonderful!"

Ray packed the tools away while Linda and I walked through the grass back to the car, visiting. A sweet, twittering bird song in a nearby fruit tree caught my attention.

"Look!" I said, pointing. "The bird found us all the way over here!"

The others looked up in amazement. She had followed us for hundreds of yards, and for the first time had burst into song.

Linda had a look of wonder on her face as the bird continued to sing. "Mary, what do you make of all of this?"

I paused for a moment. Behind her I could see a thousand trees lined up in neat rows and columns, putting oxygen back into the air for my lungs to inhale. The trees formed a living *senninbari* that would nourish me and protect me from disease. Here we were, on sacred land, ceremonially giving the land back to Mother Earth. There was no doubt in my mind as I looked back at Linda.

"I think this is the spirit of Mama-san. I feel her spirit with me every time I come here. She has returned to offer her blessings."

Certain of this, I took a deep, sweet breath.

Afterword

Tom Brokaw, the famous journalist, called Americans from my era "the greatest generation." We didn't set out to be great; we were merely born at the right time, and in the right circumstances. Mostly, the world made us who we became.

I lived through the Great Depression, the horrors of World War II, the internment of Japanese Americans, the taboo of an interracial marriage, and many other personal challenges. Of course, I also enjoyed the fruits of technology and the wonders of the modern era. If I survived the difficulties better than some of my peers, it is largely thanks to the wisdom of my mother, as well as the strength of my father.

Being called a "Jap" as a third-grader was a seminal moment for me. It was the first of many such jarring moments in my life, culminating in the atrocities of the internment. Healing from these emotional wounds was a lifelong struggle that made me who I am today.

Each of us must inevitably face the rejection of others. I realize now that it was the kindness of many people, especially those in positions of power that helped me rediscover my self-esteem and gave me the strength to face other challenges.

In living for a long time, I have witnessed the ebb and flow of events, and can take comfort in knowing that disappointments, heartbreaks, and even tragedies will look different with the passage of time. I see my own life in the context of the larger flow of humanity, which will continue to thrive long after I am gone. I feel at peace in this knowledge.

In reflecting upon Mama-san's life, I realize how much I share of her beliefs and values. While Mama-san gave me a head start by sharing her wisdom with me, it was only through developing my own that I became like her.

Bibliography and Resources

Albom, Mitch. *Tuesdays with Morrie: An old man, a young man, and life's greatest lesson.* New York, NY: Doubleday, 1997.

Andrews, Cecile. *Slow is Beautiful: New visions of community, leisure and joie de vivre.* Gabriola Island, British Columbia: New Society Publishers, 2006.

Brokaw, Tom. *The Greatest Generation.* New York, NY: Random House, 2004.

Chappell, Captain Paul K. *The End of War.* Westport, CT: Easton Studio Press, 2010.

Compassion & Choices, compassionanddying.org, Denver, Colorado.

Coombs Lee, Barbara. *Compassion in Dying: Stories of dignity and choice.* Troutdale, OR: NewSage Press, 2003.

Dominguez, Joe and Robin, Vicki. *Your Money Or Your Life: Transforming your relationship with money and achieving financial independence.* New York, NY: Penguin Books, 1992

Ford, Jamie. *Hotel on the Corner of Bitter and Sweet.* New York, NY: Ballantine Books, 2009.

Gallico, Paul. *The Snow Goose.* New York, NY: The Curtis Publishing Co., 1941; Alfred A. Knopf, Inc., 1988.

Gruenewald, Mary Matsuda. *Looking Like the Enemy: My story of imprisonment in Japanese-American internment camps.* Troutdale, OR: NewSage Press, 2005.

Gruenewald, Mary Matsuda and Michelson, Maureen R. *Young Reader's Edition of Looking Like the Enemy: My story of imprisonment in Japanese-American internment camps.* Troutdale, OR: NewSage Press, 2010.

Kashiwagi, Hiroshi. *Swimming in the American: A memoir and selected writings.* San Mateo, CA: Asian American Curriculum Project, 2005.

McCullough, Dennis M.D. *My Mother, Your Mother: Embracing "slow medicine," the compassionate approach to caring for your aging loved ones.* New York, NY: HarperCollins Publishers, 2008.

Neal, Mary C. M.D. *To Heaven and Back: The true story of a doctor's extraordinary walk with God.* Lexington, KY: Self published, 2012.

Neiwert, David A. *Strawberry Days: How internment destroyed a Japanese American community.* New York, NY: Palgrave Macmillan, 2005.

Okada, John. *No-No Boy.* Seattle, WA and San Francisco, CA: University of Washington Press, 1976.

Oliver, Mary. *Dream Work.* New York, NY: Atlantic Monthly Press,1986.

Orfali, Robert. *Death with Dignity: The case for legalizing physician-assisted dying and euthanasia.* Minneapolis, MN: Mill City Press, Inc., 2011.

Palmer, Parker J. *Let Your Life Speak: Listening for the voice of vocation.* San Francisco, CA: John Wiley & Sons, Inc., 2000.

Parker, Rebecca Ann and Hardies, Robert. *Blessing the World: What can save us now.* Boston, MA: Skinner House Books, 2006.

Weglyn, Michi. *Years of Infamy: The untold story of America's concentration camps.* New York, NY: Morrow Quilt Paperbacks, 1976.

Woodroffe, Pamela J. *Vashon Island's Agricultural Roots: Tales of the tilth as told by island farmers.* Lincoln, NE: Writers Club Press, 2002.

Mary Matsuda Gruenewald holding one of the family's strawberry carriers used in the fields.

About the Author

*M*ary Matsuda Gruenewald turned 88 years young on the eve of the publication of her third book in February 2013. Mary first began writing seriously in her 70s, realizing she wanted to tell the story of her imprisonment in Japanese-American concentration camps during World War II. As she explained, "I was no longer willing to remain silent, locked behind the self-imposed barbed-wire fences I built around my experiences in the camps."

In 2005, Mary celebrated her 80th birthday and the publication of her first book, *Looking Like the Enemy: My Story of Imprisonment in Japanese-American Internment Camps.* Her first book received high praise for its honesty and personal detailed account of confinement in these camps. Students use her book in universities, colleges, and high schools nationally. The American Library Association nominated *Looking Like the Enemy* for its list of "Best Books for Young Adults."

In 2010, Mary collaborated with her editor and publisher, Maureen R. Michelson, to adapt her adult memoir for a Young

Reader's audience. Mary explains, "My hope is to reach as many people as possible with my story about this difficult time in U.S. history and the mistreatment of Japanese Americans." Now, young students in classrooms nationwide are reading Mary's young reader's edition as a way to learn about World War II and how this war affected Japanese Americans— a chapter in U.S. history long kept hidden.

Mary's remarkable life story has been included in books and news stories. Her story was featured in the National Geographic book *Denied, Detained, Deported: Stories from the Dark Side of American Immigration* by Ann Bausum.

Mary has published articles on the Japanese-American internment and she has been interviewed by major newspapers and broadcast media, including the BBC and the Seattle Times. In addition, Mary received an Asian American Living Pioneer Award in 2003.

Mary worked as a registered nurse for more than twenty-eight years. She lives in Seattle, and still visits her family's land on Vashon, which she and her family have returned to its natural state as a forest. Mary considers this forest her legacy for future generations of all life. With the completion of her third book, Mary has decided to now learn how to play the guitar.

Visit Mary's web site: www.lookingliketheenemy.com

OTHER BOOKS BY
MARY MATSUDA GRUENEWALD

ADULT MEMOIR

LOOKING LIKE THE ENEMY: MY STORY OF IMPRISONMENT IN JAPANESE-AMERICAN INTERNMENT CAMPS

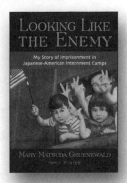

ISBN 978-0-939165-53-7

$15.00, INCLUDES PHOTOGRAH, 240 PAGES

"...a valuable contribution to the literature of Japanese-American internment...This narrative of imprisonment is painfully honest."

—**DAVID GUTTERSON,** *Snow Falling on Cedars*

When Mary Matsuda Gruenewald was seventeen years old, she and her family were evacuated to a concentration camp for Japanese Americans, along with nearly 120,000 other people of Japanese ancestry living on the West Coast. She captures the emotional and psychological essence of growing up in the midst of this profound dislocation and injustice.

YOUNG READER'S EDITION

LOOKING LIKE THE ENEMY: MY STORY OF IMPRISONMENT IN JAPANESE-AMERICAN INTERNMENT CAMPS

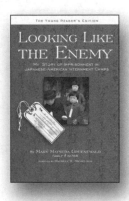

ISBN 978-0-939165-58-2

264 PAGES, $14.95

"History comes poignantly to life through the eyes of a young Japanese-American girl who is imprisoned with her family in U.S. internment camps during World War II. Vivid, heartbreaking, a true story that must never be forgotten."

—**BRENDA PETERSON,** *I Want to Be Left Behind*

This Young Reader's Edition of Mary Matsuda Gruenewald's adult memoir introduces younger readers to U.S. history through the details of this personal and riveting story. Includes historic photos, author interview, a Teacher's and Reader's Guide, Students' Writing and Research Activities, glossary of Japanese terms, and a glossary of vocabulary words.

Other Books by NewSage Press

Looking Like the Enemy: My Story of Imprisonment in Japanese-
American Internment Camps
Adult Memoir by Mary Matsuda Gruenewald

Young Reader's Edition of Looking Like the Enemy: My Story of
Imprisonment in Japanese-American Internment Camps
Young Reader's edition by Mary Matsuda Gruenewald,
Adapted by Maureen R. Michelson

One Woman One Vote: Rediscovering the Woman's Suffrage Movement
Edited by Marjorie Spruill Wheeler

Jailed for Freedom: American Women Win the Vote
By Doris Stevens, Edited by Carol O'Hare

Polar Dream: The First Solo Expedition by a Woman and Her Dog to the
Magnetic North Pole
By Helen Thayer

Women & Work: In Their Own Words
By Maureen R. Michelson

For a complete list of NewSage Press titles visit our website
www.newsagepress.com
or request information from NewSage Press

NewSage Press
PO Box 607, Troutdale, OR 97060-0607

Phone toll free: 877-695-2211
Email: info@newsagepress.com
Distributed to bookstores by Publishers Group West (Perseus)